P9-DEU-723

# Mary Jane

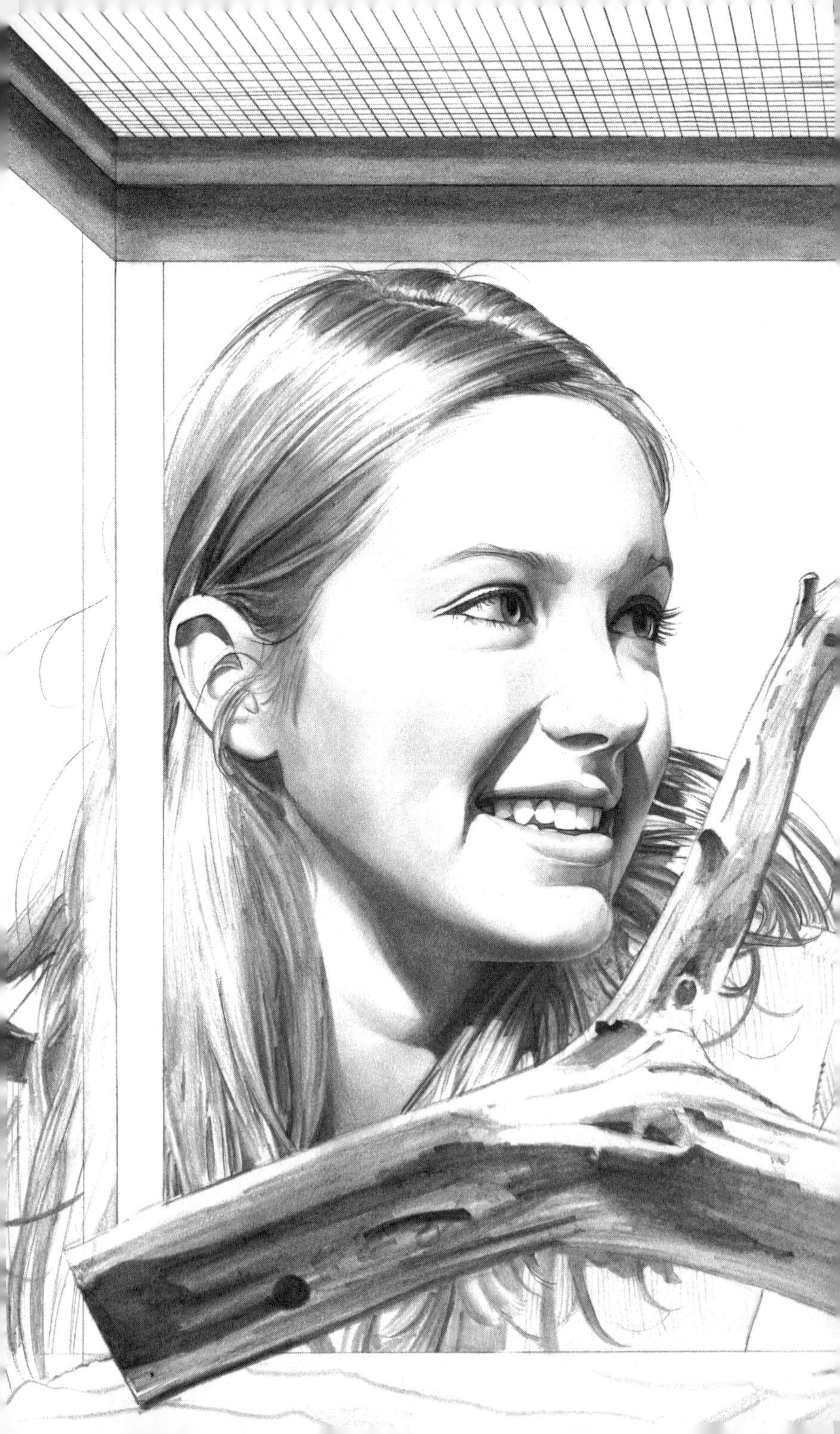

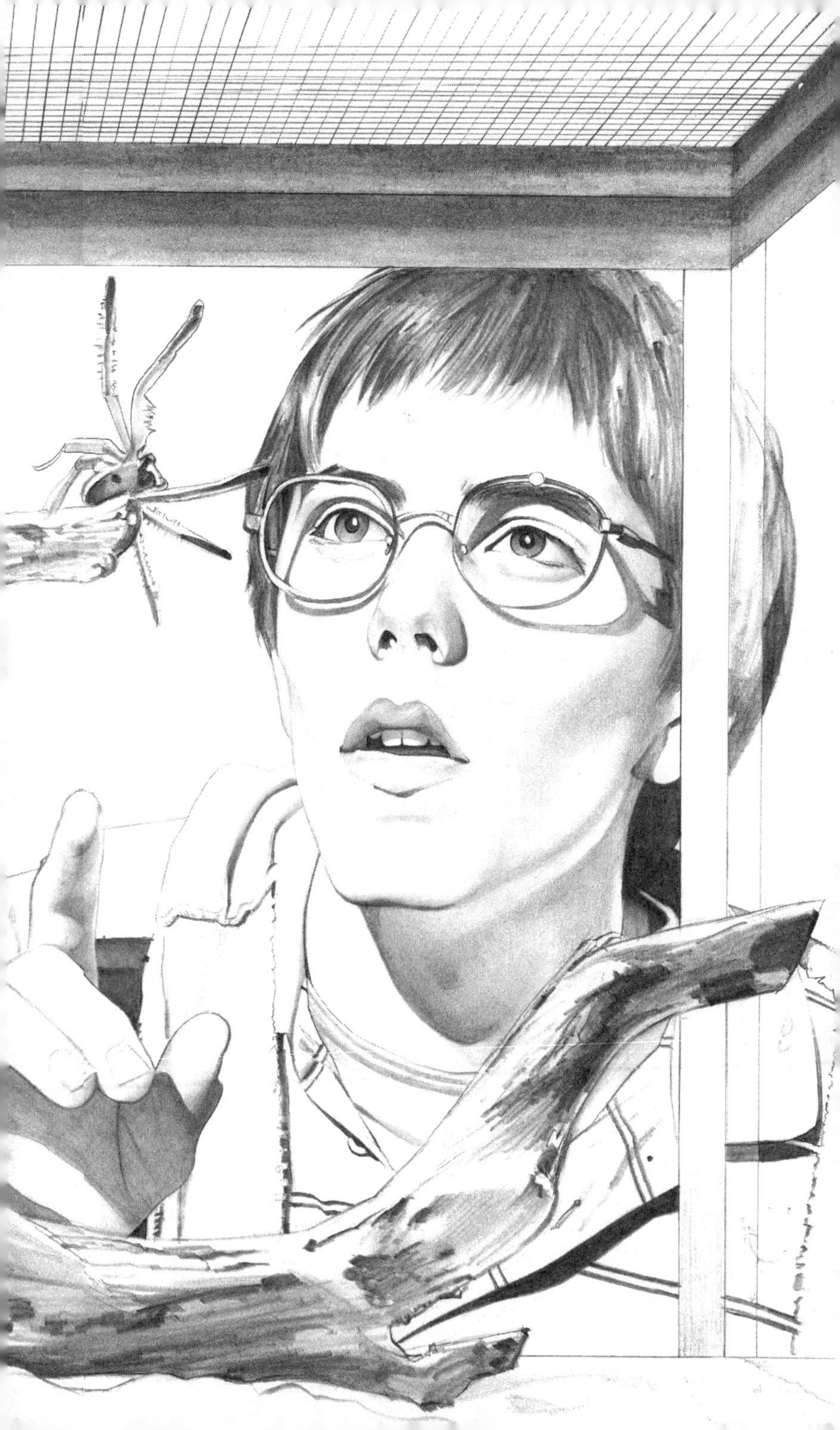

MARVEL

ULTIMATE SPIDER-MAN

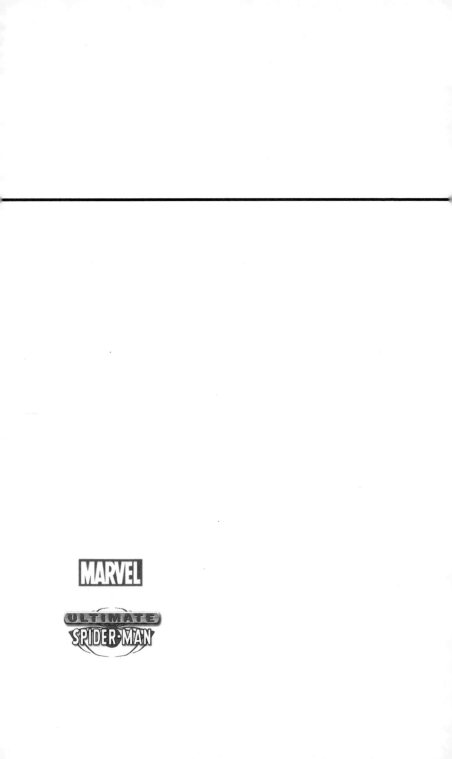

# Mary Jane

a novel by
**Judith O'Brien**

with illustrations by
Mike Mayhew

Marvel Entertainment
Group, Inc.

# MARVEL ENTERPRISES, INC.

| | |
|---|---|
| CEO & GENERAL COUNSEL | Allen Lipson |
| CHIEF CREATIVE OFFICER | Avi Arad |
| PRESIDENT & CEO, TOY BIZ | Alan Fine |
| EVP-OPERATIONS & CIO | Gui Karyo |
| CHIEF FINANCIAL OFFICER | Ken West |
| EVP-SALES, TOY BIZ | Ralph Lancelotti |
| VP-HUMAN RESOURCES | Mary Sprowls |

## PUBLISHING GROUP

| | |
|---|---|
| PRESIDENT & COO-PUBLISHING, CONSUMER PRODUCTS & NEW MEDIA | Bill Jemas |
| EDITOR IN CHIEF | Joe Quesada |
| MANAGING EDITOR | David Bogart |
| DIRECTOR OF OPERATIONS | Sangho Byun |
| PRODUCTION DIRECTOR | Dan Carr |
| DIRECTOR OF MARKETING | Peter Mathews |
| MARKETING COMMUNICATIONS MANAGER | Michael Doran |
| MANUFACTURING PRODUCT SPECIALIST | Fred Pagan |
| MANUFACTURING MANAGER | Christine Slusarz |
| MANUFACTURING REPRESENTATIVE | Stefano Perrone, Jr. |
| ART DIRECTOR/BOOK DESIGNER | Matty Ryan |
| COVER DESIGNER | Jamie Borsellino |
| EDITOR | Jennifer Lee |

## ADVERTISING—PROMOTION—RETAIL SALES

| | |
|---|---|
| EVP-CONSUMER PRODUCTS PROMOTIONS & MEDIA SALES | Russell A. Brown |
| TRADE BOOK SALES MANAGER | Jennifer Beemish |
| ADVERTISING SALES | Sara Beth Schrager |

TM & © 2003 Marvel Characters, Inc. All rights reserved. No part of this book may be reproduced in any form or by a electronic or mechanical means, including information storage and retrieval systems, without permission in writing fro the publisher, except in the case of brief quotations used in reviews.

First Edition

**MARY JANE.** First printing 2003. ISBN# 0-7851-1308-8. Published by MARVEL COMICS, a division of MARVEL ENTERTAINMENT GRO INC. OFFICE OF PUBLICATION: 10 East 40th Street, New York, NY 10016. Copyright © 2003 Marvel Characters, Inc. All rights reserv $14.99 per copy in the U.S. and $24.00 in Canada (GST #R127032852); Canadian Agreement #40668537.  All characters featured in t publication and the distinctive names and likenesses thereof, and all related indicia are trademarks of Marvel Characters, Inc. No simila between any of the names, characters, persons, and/or institutions in this publication with those of any living or dead person or institut is intended, and any such similarity which may exist is purely coincidental. **Printed in the U.S.A.** STAN LEE, Chairman Emeritus. For inf mation regarding advertising in Marvel Comics or on Marvel.com, please contact Russell Brown, Executive Vice President, Consum Products, Promotions and Media Sales at 212-576-8561 or rbrown@marvel.com

Library of Congress Control Number: 2003104192

10 9 8 7 6 5 4 3 2 1

*For anyone who has
ever gone to high school*

# prologue

At the age of nine, Mary Jane Watson had already become a master of self-distraction.

Within the Watson apartment were the usual sounds of her parents arguing. Mary Jane couldn't hear the precise words, but that didn't really matter. It was no doubt the same argument, about her dad's insufficient salary, which would usually escalate into accusations of terrible things on both sides.

Her mother, Madeline Watson, was not an easy person to please. And her dad, Philip Watson, no longer tried to please her.

Mary Jane stretched out, stomach-down, on her bed. She crossed her ankles, tapped the tip of her pen lightly against her lip. Her eyes idly scanned her room, cozy and warm, with pink curtains and a wicker chair piled with stuffed animals. It was late afternoon, and she could hear the rush-hour traffic on Park Avenue below, the horns honking, the occasional shouts and whistles of cab hailers.

A smile flickered across her lips. She was already on a new topic in her mind. It was, after all, the only way to survive her mother's moods. And her partner in those gentle games of survival was usually her father, who, with a wink or a funny face could always make even the most unpleasant situations almost okay.

With a sigh she returned her full attention to the thick blank pages before her.

"Dear Diary," she began. "Today was my first day as an official fourth grader. Amanda's in my class (yuck), and I found out that I have to work on a science project with Peter Parker (double yuck). But Sally invited me to her birthday party next week. I'm looking forward to going, even though Mom yelled at Daddy for not spending enough on the present when he took me shopping. I'll write more later."

Slamming shut the red leather diary and recapping the pen, she turned her attention to a book she had just taken out from the library. It was a lavish coffee-table book consisting of beautiful photos of a Russian ballet company. She flipped through the pictures slowly, savoring every detail of the dancers at practice, of their muscled legs and sky-high extensions, of the magnificent costumes, of glorious performances in every vibrant color imaginable.

"How lucky they are," she sighed. And then she stood up and grabbed her ballet bag. It was time for her lesson.

All she wanted to do was to sneak out of the house without being drawn into her parents' fight. She tied her shoelaces and listened to the rise and fall of their voices. From experience she knew the best time to make a break: when they were shouting, when they wouldn't hear the front door open and close.

"Some provider you turned out to be," her mother hissed.

"And I'm sure you'd be living in Windsor Castle if you hadn't dropped the baton in that Miss Tennessee pageant you're always going on about."

"If anyone dropped the baton, it was you!"

Very quietly, tiptoeing down the carpeted hall-way, Mary Jane Watson slipped out of the apartment, and walked briskly to the make-believe world of her ballet class.

\* \* \*

Mary Jane hugged her books to her chest as she entered her fourth grade science class. She hated being late to class, but her parents had been yelling all night, and she overslept her alarm clock. Even though they only lived a few blocks from the elite Bradford School, she would be marked tardy.

"Miss Watson," said Mr. Dooley, peering over his horn rimmed glasses. "How nice of you to join us."

"I'm sorry, Mr. Dooley," she apologized with such obvious sincerity that the crusty science teacher—whom many claimed was old enough to have been Teddy Roosevelt's roommate in college—actually offered something resembling a smile.

"Very well, Miss Watson. Please take your seat over there, with Mr. Parker."

"Yuck," she said only in her mind as she walked over to the table in the corner where he sat alone.

Peter Parker, the class nerd.

Actually, there was no need to limit him to the one class. He was the school nerd, acknowledged by the entire student body as totally hopeless. It was the one thing everyone agreed upon. He was pale and skinny, as if he lived his life underground, safely removed from the sun. Although everyone had to wear a uniform, Peter Parker alone had a unique ability to make even the simple dress shirt, trousers and blazer look disheveled and mismatched.

Perhaps it was his hair, which always seemed in need of a cut without actually being too long. Or his glasses, which were perpetually held together with safety pins or wads of white tape. Maybe it was the fact that he threw up during an all-school assembly in third grade, thus earning the nicknames "Pukey Parker" and "Vomit-Man."

Above all, Peter Parker was a loner. He came to school alone. He left alone. He was the last kid picked in gym for any team, last picked when special projects required partners. He ate alone in the lunchroom, and always seemed to make an effort at not being noticed, at not drawing attention to himself.

As Mary Jane approached, he jumped up. His knees

hit the table, knocking a plastic beaker of blue water to the floor.

"Mr. Parker," the teacher said blandly. "Do you wish to say something? Perhaps visit the men's room?"

"No, I..." he grabbed a handful of paper towels from the counter behind him. "I was just..." He blotted up the spill and fumbled with the beaker. For a moment he just stood, and Mr. Dooley pointed to a waste paper basket. "Oh, yes. Of course," he stepped over to it, kicking it loudly before tossing in the damp paper towels. Then he returned to his seat.

"Hello, Mary Jane," he grinned, pushing up his glasses.

"Hi," she said without looking at him. From across the classroom she could hear Amanda Peterson giggling.

"Now, ladies and gentlemen," Mr. Dooley began. "As I was saying, today we begin the exciting process that will culminate in the Bradford School Science Fair..."

"Hey, Mary Jane," Peter whispered. "I have some ideas about what we can do! Really, we can..."

"Shush," Mary Jane hissed.

"Miss Watson? Do you have something to share with the class?"

"No, Mr. Dooley." She felt her entire face turn bright red and hot.

"Well then, could you please refrain from your private conversation with Mr. Parker until I finish my instructions? You may very well find them informative, Miss Watson."

"Yes, sir," she said softly, her voice cracking in humiliation.

"I thank you." Then Mr. Dooley continued.

Mary Jane stared straight ahead, wondering how on earth she would ever survive fourth grade. More specifically, how on earth would she ever survive working side-by-side with Pukey Parker?

\* \* \*

Their heads were so close together, they were almost touching. His light brown hair seemed to blend with her auburn curls as they worked in unison.

"Hey, MJ," Peter Parker glanced up, his face inches from hers. "How about if we twist these two wires together? It won't alter the performance, but it might look a little better."

"Great idea," she beamed. "Actually, it will look nice, the blue and the green together."

"Yeah. Just like Amanda Peterson's socks."

Mary Jane laughed. "You noticed them too! I can't believe she wore those things. You know, she's in my ballet class."

"Really?" Peter frowned. He stood up and flipped on another light in his parent's basement before kneeling beside her again. In the three and a half weeks they had been working on the science fair project, they had turned his family's Forest Hills, Queens home into their own private lab. Of course they still allowed his father, Dr. Richard Parker, most of the basement for his own laboratory. After all, he was a famous scientist and was working on some big secret discovery.

Still, he was nice enough to give their project the priority until the science fair was over.

"It's taken me over ten years to get this formula to the state where it is now," he had laughed when first clearing space for the kids. "A few weeks won't matter."

The only rule in the Parker household, at least the most important rule, was not to erase Dr. Parker's formula in progress from the blackboard. Everything else, within reason, was okay, or at least open to discussion.

How Mary Jane envied Peter! No arbitrary rules, no topics off-limits. And best of all, no parents bickering over money. His parents listened to him, to them. His mom was there when they came in after school, offering something to eat and asking how their day at school had been.

And Peter Parker himself was so very different at home than he was at school. Here he was funny and smart, and although still a klutz, his clumsiness was met with kindness instead of derision.

"Amanda Peterson's really in your ballet class?" He shook his head, adjusting a battery plug on the project. "I just can't imagine that. Is she any good?"

Mary Jane paused. "Well, everyone in the class has to be good." She blushed and looked down, and Peter gently nudged her. "What I mean is it's an advanced class, so we've all been taking lessons for a while. And the Manhattan School of Ballet is one of the best schools around. But she doesn't seem to really love it the way most of us do."

"What do you mean?"

"With her, it's more like a competition."

"Lots of people are like that." His voice trailed off. "Mary Jane?"

"Hm?" She twisted the wires together.

"Did you know you have little freckles on the bridge of your nose?"

She glanced up at him. "Did you know you have a safety pin holding your glasses together?"

He grinned, and suddenly Mary Jane felt like crying. She wasn't sure why exactly. It wasn't a sad feeling, but something new and inexplicable, like having a hard lump in her throat and a strange, warm sensation spreading through her. What was it?

Swallowing, she sniffed and looked down.

"Hey, are you okay?" His voice was soft, full of concern. "You're trembling."

She shook her head, wanting him to go away or to leave her alone for a few moments, but he didn't. Instead he put a scrawny arm around her shoulders.

"You know I could probably deck you," she whispered unsteadily.

"Nope. I'm sure you could deck me."

And then, in a surprising rush, she realized why she was feeling so queasy and unfamiliar. "Peter, why are you so nice to me?"

"Because we're friends," he replied simply.

"But I was never especially nice to you. I mean, before this, before we began working on this project."

"Maybe," he said thoughtfully. Then she could hear a tinge of humor in his voice. "On the other hand, you were never especially mean to me. You never called me 'Pukey Parker.'"

"Not to your face, anyway," she closed her eyes for a moment, savoring the feel of pure friendship, the safety. "Never to your face. Vomitboy.'"

"Hey, it's Vomit-Man to you. And don't you forget it."

Mary Jane laughed weakly into his shirt, and he patted her shoulder once before his mother called from the top of the steps. "Kids! Dinner's ready!"

They jumped apart and raced for the wide wooden steps, Peter pushing her out of the way with his elbow before she ducked under his arm and beat him to the top. Breathless, they staggered into the kitchen, giggling and pushing each other.

"Calm down, you two," Mary Parker admonished with a gentle smile. "We don't want either of you to get sick before we even eat."

"Vomitboy," Mary Jane mouthed silently to Peter before saying sweetly to Mrs. Parker, "It sure smells delicious."

"It's your favorite, Mary Jane. The tuna casserole with potato chips on top."

"Oh, how wonderful!" Mary Jane answered, genuinely delighted.

"Better not eat too fast," Peter warned. "Don't want you to..."

"Peter!" Dr. Parker shouted from the kitchen door. "Enough. Hello, Mary Jane." Then he walked over to his wife and kissed her right on the lips. She flushed with pleasure, and he winked at her before rolling up his sleeves and bringing a basket of rolls to the table.

Peter didn't seem to think anything was unusual about this, about how his parents acted towards each other, how they treated their son. That they all ate dinner together every evening, a dinner his mother cooked herself, followed by brownies or little pieces of fruit with coconut on top or something else marvelous and sweet.

A full plate was handed to her. "Thank you, Mrs. Parker," Mary Jane said taking a sip of milk that wasn't quite cold but delicious nonetheless. The big kitchen was out of date, like the rest of the house, and the refrigerator even had a funny thing on top that Dr. Parker called an old-fashioned turret. The floors sloped; the carpets in the rest of the house were worn in spots. Just as Peter's glasses were held together with tape and safety pins, the front door didn't close all the way unless you kicked the bottom (causing an indentation in the wood from years of shoe contact) and the upright piano was hopelessly out of tune.

Peter passed her the salad—plain iceberg lettuce, which would horrify her mother. She grinned and helped herself to a generous portion.

In short, nothing in the Parker household seemed unusual to Peter. But to Mary Jane, it was nothing short of magical.

* * *

Mary Jane and Peter stepped back from their project so everyone else could get the best view. There it sat, the fruit of weeks of labor, on a card table covered with a dark blue cloth. Some of the judges who had passed by unofficially were unable to hide their surprise and delight with the project, a two-foot tall robot named Floyd who could speak simple sentences and nod his head on command. Dr. Parker, camera in hand, snapped pictures of the creative team, Floyd, and Mrs. Parker.

"Here, honey," she brushed Mary Jane's hair off her forehead. "There, now we can see those beautiful eyes."

"They'll come," Peter said quietly when Mrs. Parker went over to see another mother, and Dr. Parker rewound the film. "I'm sure they will."

"I'm pretty sure Mom won't. Maybe Daddy will."

"That's cool," Peter said with a definite lukewarm tone. He'd only met Mrs. Watson once, but didn't like her much. She seemed like a snob. But he didn't mention what he thought. After all, he was a kid who rode the subway every day by himself from Queens. He was about the only student whose parents scrimped and saved to send him to the Bradford School for its academic reputation, not for its pedigree name.

Although he didn't care much for Mrs. Watson, he was beginning to like her daughter. A lot. It surprised him how much he started to think about her, how very much he looked forward to seeing her skip up his front steps with a big smile on her face every afternoon. And it always took him by surprise that Mary Jane Watson, by far the prettiest girl in fourth grade, if not in the entire school, was smiling at him, at Peter Parker.

Just then the door to the gymnasium opened, and she gasped. "Daddy!"

The man in the doorway was handsome and well-built. For a moment he seemed to lean sideways, as if about to enter through a mysterious hidden door. Then he straightened, his gaze unfocused.

"Merry Janie?"

Peter frowned. The man's voice was slurred, and he lurched forward, bumping into the assistant vice principal and spilling her punch. But he didn't seem to notice, nor did he notice when he pushed someone's little brother to the floor.

Mary Jane's face turned white, and she took a step backward.

Peter reached over and tried to hold her hand, but she withdrew it quickly, as if she had been scalded.

"No," she said in a low voice. "Oh, please not now. Not tonight."

Dr. Parker glanced at his wife, who shook her head in worry over what to do. Then he marched straight over to Philip Watson.

"Hello, sir," he said briskly, as if nothing unusual had happened. "I'm Richard Parker, Peter's father."

"Who?" Her father's head seemed to rotate on a bobbin.

"Richard Parker. My son Peter worked with your daughter on this project."

"What are you talking about?" Watson asked Dr. Parker. Then he saw his daughter, and as if both surprised and utterly charmed to see her, he shook himself free of Dr. Parker's gentle grasp and lunged forward. "Janie! Little Merry Janie!"

Mary Jane stood motionless, eyes wide, as if watching a horror show. And she was.

In three long, staggering steps, he crashed into the card table. The entire podium collapsed, taking Floyd the robot down in a sickening crunch of metal and floating gold paper stars.

"Hello, I am Floyd. Hello I am Frrrrrr..." The mechanical voice sputtered into oblivion as his detached head rolled against the folded bleachers.

The gymnasium went silent. And then there was one sound. Philip Watson lay in the ruins of his daughter's science project, laughing like a drunken hyena.

Peter looked at Mary Jane. She gave him one sad glance, her eyes brimming with tears, and then she ran. She ran as fast as she could through the front door her father had just stumbled through. Peter began to go after her, but his father stopped him.

"Let her go, Peter. She needs to be alone now."

* * *

*Dear Diary,*

*It's been a week since the disaster at the science fair. I found out later that after I left, Dr. Parker got a cab for Daddy and sent him home, but he never did come home that night. He still hasn't. Mom pretends like nothing's wrong, but Granny Watson keeps on calling, asking to speak to him. It's really awful.*

*Dr. and Mrs. Parker tried to keep our project still entered, since several of the judges had seen Floyd before my father killed him. But other parents protested, and not all of the judges could figure out what we had done just by looking at the pieces. Dr. Parker even tried to get his photographs developed at one of those one-hour places, so they could get an idea. But still we were not allowed to be in it.*

*I don't want to see anyone. Peter keeps calling and trying to talk to me at school, but I avoid him. He must really hate me, even though he stopped by the other day.*

*Mommy has tried to be extra nice, but she's too sad about Daddy leaving to really understand.*

*I miss him, too.*

*This is all my fault. I begged him to come to the science fair, and look what happened. Sometimes at night I wish I could die. I really do.*

\* \* \*

Peter felt he had lost his best friend. He was left confused as to what had happened, why Mary Jane had vanished so completely from his life. His parents told him to give her some more time, not to push her, for that would only push her away. Still, Peter was left to wonder what he had done.

Mary Jane felt she had lost not one, but all of her friends, her father, and in many ways, her very world. Everything had become so strange at home. She hadn't figured it out herself yet, so how could she explain it to someone else?

For the two kids who had spent so much time and energy in creating a fantastical robot named Floyd, everything crashed down in a twisted pile of rubbish. Nothing was the same.

Above all, Philip Watson never did return home. His whereabouts remained a mystery.

Mary Jane did not rant or rage or openly question what had happened, or why. Instead she simply withdrew into a world of her own making. Sometimes she would hear her mother yelling or pleading with someone on the phone. Her father? Her grandmother? She never knew, and in a way, did not wish to know.

Rather than ponder the unanswerable she immersed herself in ballet lessons. In fact, she even took extra ballet classes at the Manhattan School of Ballet. And after her own classes ended she would watch the older girls, budding ballerinas all, with their lithe frames and tightly wound buns at the napes of their slender necks. Some nights she would take four back-to-back classes and come home exhausted, barely able to keep her eyes open to do her homework.

But it was worth it, to escape into a world of make-believe, to have nothing more pressing than the next step, or the music, or dancing in unison with the other girls in her class. The hours at ballet became her favorite moments, the only times she felt in control of her life.

Then Mary Jane noticed some pieces of furniture were missing from home. At first she thought the living room had just been rearranged, as her mom had done in the past. But when the sofa vanished, and was not replaced by a more expensive model, she realized something was very wrong. Then a side table was gone, and the big buffet in the dining room. One by one pieces of crystal and silverware disappeared.

They were all gone, just as her father had disappeared. And with just as little explanation.

Finally she tried to ask her mother about what was happening. About the vanished father and furniture. And painfully she asked if she—Mary Jane—had anything to do with the sudden change in their lives.

"Of course not, honey!" her mother said distractedly. That was the only answer Mary Jane received. The more she heard it, the less reassured she felt.

On the night of Mary Jane's dance recital, her mom failed to even remember the event, much less get dressed and make an appearance. She was spending more hours of her day in bed. So while the other girls' parents waited in the wings with bouquets of roses, Mary Jane danced the lead in the "Swan Lake" segment, performing for only herself.

For a moment, with the glare of the footlights obscuring her gaze, she thought she saw Peter Parker in one of the back rows. In fact, she could have sworn it was Peter, his glasses reflecting the light back at her. But when the houselights came back on, the seat she thought he had been in was empty.

The next morning at school Peter was called out of class by the principal.

Mr. Dooley left the room next, and everyone could hear hushed whispers in the hallway. Mary Jane's hands clenched into fists, and a terrible thud seemed to land in her middle. Something was very, very wrong.

Then Mr. Dooley reentered the room. He had a strange expression on his face, not the usual arched eyebrows or slightly amused disdain. For a long moment he simply stood at the front podium. Then he took off his glasses and wiped them with his handkerchief.

"Ladies and gentlemen," he said at last, folding the handkerchief with great deliberation and placing it back into his suit pocket. "I have some tragic news."

"Mr. Parker's parents..." Then his voice softened. "Peter's parents, Dr. and Mrs. Parker, were both killed this morning in a plane crash. They were on their way to Switzerland to attend a conference and..."

Mr. Dooley's voice became a buzz, a droning, unintelligible noise to her. She remained at her desk, her spine rigid against the back of her chair.

Dr. and Mrs. Parker. Peter's parents.

Some people were looking at Mary Jane. Had she made a noise? Did she say something?

Dr. and Mrs. Parker.

She had a vision of Mrs. Parker dishing out the casserole, of Dr. Parker winking at her. She saw Peter laughing when his dad rustled his hair, then smiling at Mary Jane.

She stood up, her books tumbling to the floor.

"Miss Watson? Do you have something to say?" Mr. Dooley asked.

She shook her head. "Where is he, sir? Where is Peter?"

"He's downstairs in the office. An aunt or uncle is with him at the present time."

Mary Jane simply walked out of the room.

"Miss Watson!" She heard Mr. Dooley call. But the door swung shut behind her, and she was in the hall, running to the principal's office. Her shoes echoed in the empty corridor, a hollow, lonely sound.

And then she was at the principal's office. She did not hesitate to open the door.

But only the secretary was there, seated behind an oversized desk.

"Yes?" The secretary's eyes were reddened, and she blinked at Mary Jane. A box of tissues was in her hand, the designer kind made to look like wood or something.

What a strange thing to notice, Mary Jane thought to herself.

"Excuse me." Her voice sounded so weird, even to her own ears. "Where is Peter? Peter Parker?"

"Oh, honey. They took him home. His uncle came here and took him home." She slumped over and began to sob. "That poor kid. That poor little kid."

Mary Jane backed out of the office. And for a long while, it seemed, she simply stood in the hall.

And then she felt her own eyes sting as if prickled by a thousand tiny needles. "Peter," she said softly. "I'm so, so sorry." She, too, began to sob.

* * *

*Dear Diary,*

*Today was Dr. and Mrs. Parker's funeral. I went all by myself on the subway, and was the only kid from the whole school at the funeral. All these people were there, hundreds it seemed. Lots of them spoke in foreign accents, and said how very important Dr. Parker's work was, how he would be missed by the scientific world. I met Peter's Uncle Ben and Aunt May, who seem nice but really old. I overheard someone say they will both move into his parent's house so that Peter can live in his own home. Then someone else said that his uncle and aunt could not afford to pay for private school, so Peter won't be coming back to Bradford. I handed him a card, one of those sympathy things with gold letters they sell at the drug store. But he barely seemed to recognize me.*

*Mom says we have to move into a smaller place since Granny Watson is 'cutting her off.' I know I have no right to feel sorry for myself, especially after what happened to Peter, to his parents, but I'm scared to leave. I wonder if there is really a heaven, and if Dr. and Mrs. Parker are together now, laughing. But they should be here with Peter, laughing in the kitchen. It just isn't right.*

*Those times I spent with the Parkers were like heaven. I just didn't realize it at the time.*

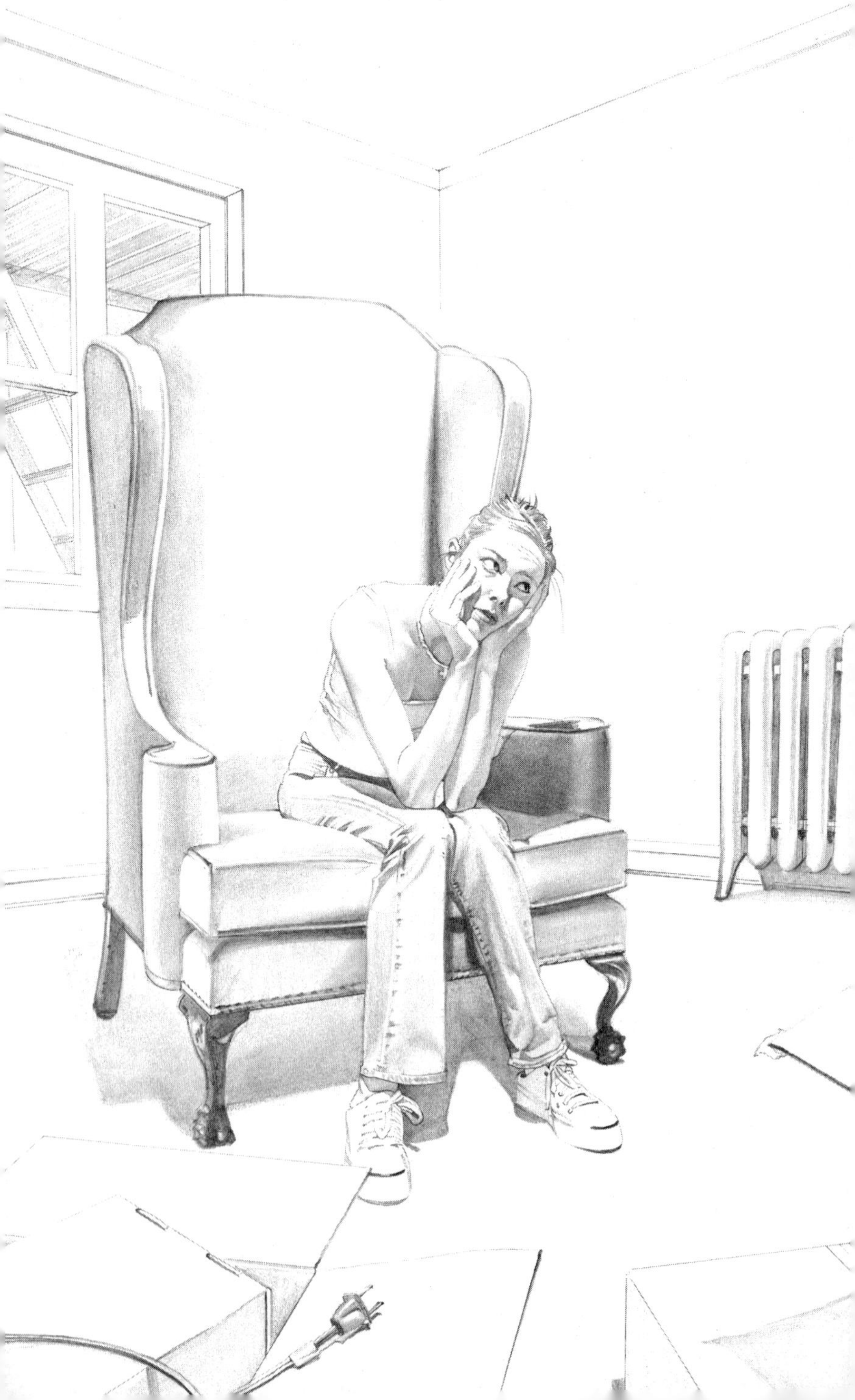

# chapter 1

**Six years later...**

Mary Jane straightened from her bent position over the cardboard box and rubbed a hand over the small of her back. It was with great reluctance that she stood up, for now she was faced with yet another view of the dismal apartment that defined her new life. And this one was no improvement over the previous panoramas.

"Is the extension cord in that box?" Her mother stepped into the living room, her freshly home-colored hair peeking from beneath a triangle of French provincial fabric. It used to be part of an elegant table linen set, purchased long ago. But she had put the cloth to work three apartments ago as curtains, a makeshift sofa cover, a disastrous attempt at a wall hanging inspired by a Martha Stewart segment on morning TV, and finally an assortment of rags.

"Nope," Mary Jane took a deep breath and exhaled slowly. "The extension cord is probably still in with the Christmas tree lights."

Outside, the shrill pierce of a siren came and then faded. A truck rumbled by, rattling the lamps and windows, followed by a car alarm and a loud, impatient honk. Her mother smiled weakly. "I guess we'll get used to that."

"Sure."

"We're so close to the subway here, and the bus stop is right on the corner. We certainly don't need a car."

Mary Jane nodded.

"This is really the up-and-coming borough, you know. No one lives in Manhattan anymore; they're all flocking to Queens. I hear they're getting a Starbucks down the street. Did you see on the corner, the sign for a Gap? You love those clothes. At least you used to love those clothes, all the turtlenecks and jeans. And Mike says the high school is really great," her mother continued without waiting for any sort of reply. Whenever she became slightly agitated, her Hickory Hollow, Tennessee accent became more pronounced, a jarring contrast to her carefully honed exterior. "You always make friends so easily. Remember how nervous you were at the last school? Then, by the second week, you came home with all those nifty gals. Mike says you have a real gift for making friends."

Mike, Mary Jane thought. Great. Her mom's boyfriend thinks she has a gift for friendship, as if he would know anything. Mike was okay-looking, she had to admit. But there was something about him she didn't like, didn't trust.

"I know you're not crazy about Mike, hon. But he's really attentive. Sweet in his own way. He may be rough in spots. Heck, most spots. And he's...well. I don't know. Since your father left and everything," she straightened. "Hey, didn't one of your little friends from Bradford live here in Queens?"

"Yes." She did not want to talk. She was too tired from the move, from the utterly depressing place she would now call home. From the sound of yet another car alarm.

Problem was, she had really liked the last school, the one in Greenwich Village. But her mother said the apartment was too expensive to keep. Mary Jane suspected that her mom was just using that as an excuse to move closer to Mike, but that probably wasn't fair.

Her mother kept chattering away, a new nervous habit that was proving to be much more irritating than her previous spaced-out silences. "What was his name? That boy from Queens you used to spend so much time with. He was a skinny little kid, right? Smart, though. I do remember he was smart. His parents divorced or his father had an affair or something."

"His parents were killed in a plane crash."

"Was that it? I knew it was something like that."

Yeah. Right, Mom. Being killed in a plane crash is just like having an affair.

"Now don't get all sullen on me, Missy," her mother

25

admonished. "Mike is coming over with a pizza. Won't that be fun?"

I'll try to contain my excitement.

"That's great, Mom," she said instead.

"What was his name again?"

"Whose name?"

"Oh, for heaven's sake, Mary Jane. The name of the skinny little boy with the dead parents."

"Peter." Mary Jane swallowed. When was the last time she had said his name aloud? "His name was Peter Parker."

"That's right. Now I remember." Looking around, her mother placed her hands on her hips with feigned satisfaction. "I really think this place will be cute, don't you?"

Yeah, Mom. It'll be a regular Barbie playhouse.

Mary Jane nodded.

"Do you think we should put the Queen Ann chair by the window or in front of the radiator?"

The Queen Ann wing chair, the only piece of furniture remaining from the Park Avenue apartment, stood like a deposed monarch in the center of the room, its graceful legs nicked and scarred by the unexpected abuse it had been forced to endure during the past few years. Mary Jane knew how it felt, the constant uprooting, and the sense of a temporary existence. And now it would be forced to sit before a radiator.

How long would they stay here, in this Forest Hills flat? Where would they be in a year, even six months?

It wasn't that Mary Jane lacked compassion for her

mother and the difficulties she had faced since Philip Watson left. Of course it must have been hard, even humiliating, to realize that all of her former friends abandoned her the moment her social and economic status plunged. Granny Watson had helped in her own remote way, paying Mary Jane's Bradford tuition for a couple of years, allowing them to remain in the Manhattan apartment for a while. But finally she decided it was time for Madeline to, as she phrased it, "stand on your own two feet." And with a glance at her granddaughter, amended it to four feet. She didn't mean to be unkind; she was just unable to place herself in their position.

Mary Jane didn't mind when she was forced to attend public schools. In fact, it was a relief to escape from all of those sneering kids, the parents who would pretend to be so kind and concerned, but who really just wanted to get whatever details they could repeat later over cocktails.

"Why, if it isn't little Mary Jane Watson! I haven't seen your mother for simply ages. And you're every bit as pretty as she is. Where has she been keeping herself, dearest?"

No, Mary Jane didn't mind leaving the Bradford School, although she would miss some of the teachers. And a few of the kids. What she did mind, however, was not being able to attend the Manhattan School of Ballet.

"We simply can't afford it, hon," her mother had said. "Not until we can get back on our feet. All four of them."

"If Dad hadn't left, I'd still be taking lessons there," she had murmured aloud.

"If your father hadn't left, I wouldn't be busting my back trying to keep a roof over our head. I wouldn't have had to hire Mike to track down your dad for child support payments in the first place!"

Mary Jane stared at the Queen Ann wing chair. Her mother cleared her throat. "Listen, honey. There is a dance studio a few blocks away. The prices are within our range."

"Really?" Mary Jane couldn't keep the hope from her voice. How wonderful it would be to take dance again! To lose herself in the rarefied, beautiful world of classical ballet!

"Yes. It's called Ruby's House-O-Dance, right over on Queens Boulevard."

"Ruby's House-O-Dance?"

"It sounds fabulous—you can take tap, ballroom dancing, the cha-cha, baton twirling, gymnastics—lots of great things you've never explored before. They have disco nights on Friday." She avoided meeting her daughter's eyes.

"Baton twirling?"

"And you know, more than one person has mentioned that you should really think of entering pageants."

"Pageants?"

"You know, beauty pageants. Miss America-type of stuff. The baton-twirlers always win."

"Mom, why on earth would I ever consider doing something like that?" Mary Jane asked incredulously.

"For college money," her mother replied bluntly. "Mike suggested it, said you're really a knockout. College is only a couple of years away. It will be here before you know it. And if you have any hopes of catching a husband, well, college is where you have to go. The good ones are all taken after that. And with a beauty pageant title or two, you can have your absolute pick of the men. That's how I got your father. He used to be so proud of me. I mean, back then it was really something to be a beauty queen. And your father was from such an old New York family, regular blue-bloods."

Mary Jane crossed her arms and stared at her mother. Who was this person, and how could Mary Jane possibly be related to her?

"I'm going out for a walk," Mary Jane said at last.

"Have you unpacked your room yet?"

My room? Do you mean the small cubicle overlooking the fire escape?

"Yes. It's all unpacked."

"Okay," her mother said brightly. "Have fun exploring the neighborhood. And don't forget, Mike is coming over with a pizza in just a couple of hours."

Mary Jane managed a smile and left the apartment, determined to accomplish two things. One, she would walk over to Ruby's House-O-Dance and check the place out. Who knows? Maybe it would be okay. Maybe taking lessons there would be better than no lessons at all.

And two, she would get home as late as possible, late enough to miss her mom's creepy boyfriend and his tainted pizza.

* * *

It was a situation she was growing used to, being the new kid at school. Being accustomed to it didn't make it any easier. But at least she had a rough idea of what to expect.

Luckily, her mother was unable to take her there, for it was her first day of training as a Skye Bleu Cosmetics Consultant. In other words, her mom would be selling nail polish, essential oils and pots of lipgloss door-to-door. It was an improvement over her last job as a hostess at a restaurant she had refused to patronize when they were still living on Park Ave.

Over breakfast, Mary Jane watched as her mother tapped her carefully polished nails on the table and repeatedly flipped over her wrist to check her watch for the time.

"Have a good day at school, hon," she said distractedly, tapping her foot on the blue speckled linoleum floor in the kitchen. She was on her third cup of coffee, and in the unforgiving harshness of the morning light, Mary Jane could see lines bracketing her mouth and at the corners of her eyes.

Suddenly, her mother looked old.

"You okay, Mom?"

She flashed a quick smile. "Sure. I'm just, well... When do you have to leave? Don't want to be late for your first day at your new high school." Hickory Hollow was alive and kicking in her twang.

"I have a few minutes. Are you okay?"

"It's just that it's been a while since I've really worked." She dumped her mug into the sink. "Actually, I'm just not very good at it. Who am I fooling? And this is a test, the training period. Probationary six weeks, whatever you want to call it. The bottom line is if I don't do well, if I don't measure up to their standards, I'm out of a job."

Mary Jane shifted uncomfortably, then stood up to rinse out her cereal bowl. Never before had her mother expressed such raw self-doubt. "You'll be great, Mom," she glanced over her shoulder, and her mother was staring out the window. She looked thin, tiny almost.

"I wonder if a window box would help," she mumbled, almost to herself. "Maybe something cheerful. Tulips or mums or something."

"Yeah, well. I'd better go now, Mom. Good luck. Um, you'll be great."

"Thanks, hon. And good luck at school."

With a quick wave Mary Jane was out the door, a guilty sense of relief washing over her as she stepped onto the pavement.

Midtown High School was only a few blocks away. The moment she rounded the corner and saw the aggressively urban, institutionally unattractive brick building with bars and wire over the windows, a sense of helpless dread came over her. It wasn't the unwelcoming appearance of the place that caused her to pause and bite her lip, although she did wonder briefly if the bars were to keep people from jumping out of, or from slithering into, the classrooms. Instead, it was the students themselves that freaked her out.

Everyone was clustered into groups, giggling and gossiping or just hanging out with each other. They were all wearing completely different clothes from hers; tight, funky jeans seemed to be the norm, while she was in a girly blue dress. They swept past, ignoring her, talking on their cell phones, even brushing her shoulders as they laughed their way to school. The entire population seemed to be happy and confident and, above all, they all seemed to know the exact location of their homeroom. A single bell rang, and she was the only one who jumped as if goosed by an invisible hand.

Mary Jane Watson, her spiral notebook pressed to her chest like a suit of armor, stared ahead and wondered how she would ever get the nerve to enter the building.

"Are you new here?" A dark-haired girl with enormous brown eyes stood before her.

"How could you tell?" Mary Jane blinked.

"Oh, maybe it's that look of rampaging terror in your eyes. Or the sound of your knees knocking together. Or maybe it's..."

"Enough!" She finally laughed. "Hi, I'm Mary Jane Watson, the new kid at school."

"Good to meet you," the other girl grinned. "I'm Wendy Gonzales. Former new kid at school. I've been here since September."

"How is it? I mean, do you like it?"

"Yeah, it's okay." Then Wendy motioned towards the front steps, and they both began walking. "Actually, it's better than okay. I moved here this summer from Chicago, so it took a little adjusting. But I really like it here. You have your normal cliques, of course, the jocks and the brains and the stoners and the geeks. But for the most part everyone's okay, and the school itself is really good."

"That's great to know." As they approached, Mary Jane slowed her pace. The building seemed to loom ahead, massive and solid.

"Who's your homeroom teacher?" Wendy asked.

"Just a second," Mary Jane opened her spiral notebook, her computer-printed schedule neatly taped to the inside.

"Organized. How impressive."

"Yeah, well. I had to do something last night. This kept me busy for at least a minute or two. Okay, let's see: I have Mr. Wilner for homeroom."

"Get out!" Wendy pushed her shoulder and almost dislodged her notebook. "Oh, sorry. But I have Wilner, too. We're in the same homeroom."

"That's great! So...we can walk there together?" Mary Jane looked at her hopefully.

"Nah. That would ruin my reputation. You go on ahead. I'll catch you later."

Mary Jane stood for a moment. "Oh, sure."

Then Wendy laughed. "I'm kidding! Come on."

And suddenly, right then and there, Mary Jane knew everything would be all right.

\* \* \*

By science class, eighth period, Mary Jane already recognized a few of the kids from earlier classes. Wendy was there, the third class they had together, not counting lunch. Plus there was an incredibly cute guy who came to her table at lunch.

"Oh my God," Wendy hissed as they were eating. "See that guy over there, the one with the hot body and the face of a Greek deity?"

Mary Jane looked in the general direction Wendy was not-so-subtly gesturing in. "I don't see anyone Apollo-like."

"He's at one o'clock, walking to one-oh-five."

"Wendy, what are you talking about? I don't see..." Then she stopped. "Oh my God."

Wendy nodded with satisfaction. "That, girlfriend, is Harry Osborn."

"Oh my God."

"Not only is he gorgeous, he's also the richest kid in the school. I don't mean just nice-car rich. I mean a fleet of nice cars, limo drivers, vacations in tropical islands his dad owns. That kind of rich. Note the tan. Note the sun-kissed hair."

"Is he nice?"

"Who cares?" Wendy nudged her. "I mean, really, he

could keep me entertained all day by just sitting there and jingling his Ferrari keys in my direction. I probably couldn't stand the excitement if he actually said something."

"Wow. He's absolutely..."

"Oh my God, he's coming over here! Sit straight! No, look down! Laugh as if I just said something wickedly clever."

"Wendy, he's looking at us!"

"No, he's looking at you! Damn, he's not even stopping to ogle Carrie Beckerman. Everyone stops to ogle Carrie."

Mary Jane took a sip of her soda, put it down, then fiddled with a napkin. And suddenly he was there.

"Hello, ladies," he said. His teeth were so white they seemed to glow. "How are you doing today?"

As he spoke, he stared directly at Mary Jane.

"We're great, Harry," Wendy replied in a voice that sounded as if she had just inhaled helium. "Harry Osborn, this is Wendy Gonzales."

Mary Jane almost choked. "No, YOU are Wendy Gonzales. I am Mary Jane Watson."

"Glad to meet you," he extended his hand to Mary Jane, and she shook it over her bright orange lunch tray. "Welcome to Midtown High."

"Thanks," she smiled.

"I'll see you both around school," he winked. And then he turned and walked away, allowing a perfect, unobstructed view of his rear end.

"Could he be any hotter?" Wendy gasped.

"Totally." And of course they spoke of Harry Osborn and his charms throughout the rest of lunch.

And now there he was in her science class, sitting directly behind her. She stared straight ahead, waiting for the teacher, who was fumbling with her class cards, to start attendance.

Then she felt something press against her shoulder.

"Hey, Mary Jane," Harry whispered, pushing the pink tip of his eraser into her back.

"Hey, Harry," she shot back. It was impossible not to grin with Harry Osborn a mere foot or so away.

Then the teacher began. "Good afternoon, ladies and gentlemen. We have a new student in class. Let's all welcome her. Miss Mary Jane Watson, would you please stand up?"

Mary Jane felt herself blush, but again it was all part of the new-kid-at-school drill, including the obligatory blush. Wendy applauded loudly, and Harry clapped slowly, a smirk on his handsome face.

How can he manage to make a smirk look so attractive?

She sat down as soon as possible and leaned forward, ready for class to begin.

"Very well. Now, as you all know, three quarters of this semester's grade will be dependent upon..."

The door flew open, and a tall, lanky kid with bad posture and in dire need of hair gel slunk into the class. His shirttails were untucked, his jeans worn and so long they all but covered his sneakers. Like a puppy, his feet were huge. He seemed overwhelmed by the mere task of carrying his books, and papers jutted out of his pockets and from the leaves of the books as he fumbled.

"Sorry," he mumbled to no one in particular. A few people in the class giggled.

"Please, take your seat," the teacher instructed.

He kept his head down as he walked up Mary Jane's aisle. Something about him was familiar, and she held her breath as he passed.

Then from the corner of her eye, she saw Harry casually extend a long, well-muscled leg. Before she could shout a warning, the lanky kid tripped in an almost perfectly executed pratfall. His books tumbled to the ground, papers fluttering more gently. The classroom erupted in laughter.

The boy righted himself as quickly as possible. Even the teacher was unable to suppress a smile.

Immediately Mary Jane jumped to his side and helped him gather his books and papers.

"Thanks," he muttered, his face covered by a thatch of straight brown hair.

Mary Jane stopped and read the top of one of his papers. "Peter?"

Slowly he looked up, and their eyes met. "Mary Jane?"

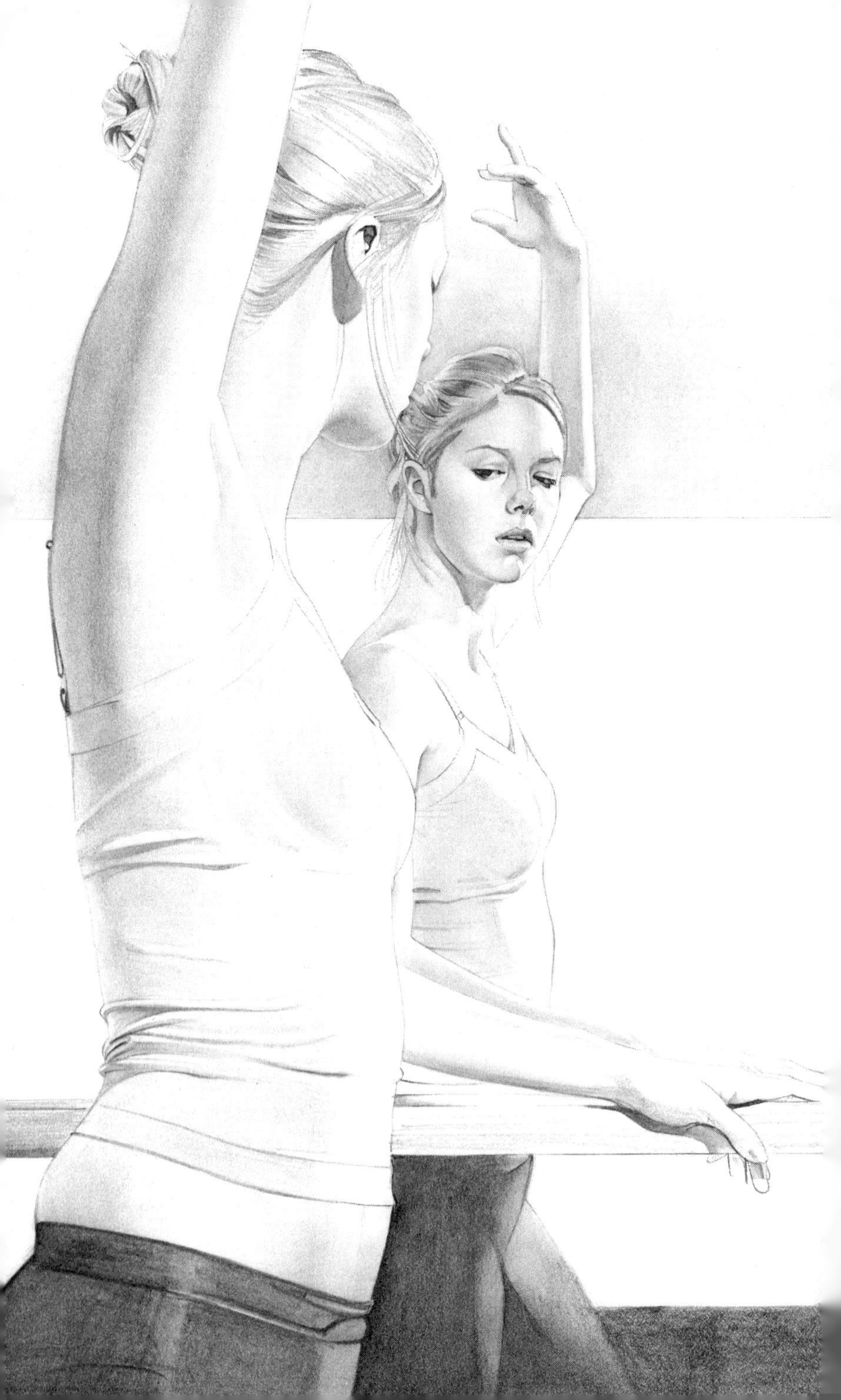

# chapter 2

*Dear Diary,*

*It's the third week of my new school, and I'm actually beginning to like it! The work itself is pretty easy, although science may be more of a challenge—and more fun—than the other classes. Plus Harry Osborn is in science, which makes the class a lot more interesting, no matter what Miss Ingram has to say. He is totally hot. I've never seen a guy like him in real life—it's almost as if he's been air-brushed and digitally enhanced.*

*Wendy Gonzales is great. I feel as if I've known her all my life. And speaking of old friends...I still can't believe Peter Parker! He's still such a sweet guy, but Wendy says he's an impossible geek and even speaking to him can ruin my cool potential. Why does he wear those Coke-bottle bottom glasses? I suppose he really doesn't care how he looks or what anyone thinks of him. Yet when I see him in the lunchroom, clutching his tray and looking for a place, anyplace, to sit, there is clearly such pain in his eyes. At least I think there's pain. It's hard to tell through the inch-thick lenses.*

*Oddly, Harry Osborn is actually friends with Peter. Okay, so Peter does his homework for him. Nice of Peter, although he doesn't seem to have much of a choice in the matter. Seems Harry is guy candy, not much of a deep thinker, as if he needs to be an Einstein. Still, at least Peter has a friend in Harry. Or something like it.*

*Mom is surviving her Skye Bleu initiation, and will soon be a salesgal.*

*Gal. Who talks like that?*

*Now off to ballet!*


Mary Jane capped her pen and slipped her diary between her mattress and boxspring, the usual hiding place. She resisted the urge to reread the previous pages in her diary, as if that would somehow jinx her into going back to how unhappy she was just a few weeks before.

But now, everything had changed!

She grabbed her ballet bag, with the tacky red, white and blue leotard and tights inside, the official uniform of Ruby's House-O-Dance. Ruby herself was an ex-Ziegfeld girl who seemed to go by the motto "there is no such thing as too much aqua eyeshadow or rose oil." Mary Jane thought she'd make a good client for her mother.

But she was enthusiastic, even if she did pepper her instruction with references to dancers who nobody young enough to still dance had ever heard of. And Ruby seemed to take an immediate shine to Mary Jane.

"Why," she said after the first lesson, "you could be

a double for Vera-Ellen!" Later she added, "Your technique reminds me of an early Ann Miller."

Ruby was a follower of the shuffle-one, change-two school of dance, which was fine for Mary Jane. The important thing was that it was dance, or at least near-dance.

"How about 'Dance Lite?'" Wendy had suggested when MJ described the classes.

So maybe it was Dance Lite. Ruby also taught baton twirling and something called "ribbon dancing," which she claimed had been very big at the New York World's Fair of 1939. Some afternoons combined modern dance with gymnastics, which meant everyone somersaulted to Ruby's "Golden Oldies" collection. Then came disco and ballroom dancing on Tuesdays, complete with a guy named Anthony in a white suit and a black silk shirt. Mary Jane thought he looked so ridiculous he was almost cool.

The only class she avoided was Ruby's exotic belly dancing, and that was more due to the Arabian Nights outfit Ruby wore than to the class itself. There was something disturbing about seeing Ruby bumping and grinding in an old "I Dream of Jeannie" costume.

By far Mary Jane's favorite night was on Wednesday, when Madame Olga from Minsk taught classical ballet. Although her technique was a far cry from the clean discipline of the Manhattan School of Ballet, she did seem to know what she was doing. She also dropped names,

Nijinsky and Pavlova and Nureyev and Balanchine and Baryshnikov, pronouncing each as if it were a savory covered dish from the Russian Tea Room.

It was during the second Madame Olga lesson that Mary Jane was on the receiving end of one of Madame's clicks.

As usual she was strolling down the barre as the students were performing their exercises. Pausing just behind Mary Jane, Madame Olga cleared her throat. Then she clicked.

Mary Jane looked over her shoulder at Madame.

Without any apology, or even any attempt at politeness, Madame pointed to Mary Jane's thighs with her cane. "Ve do not vant tubby ballerinas." Then she moved on.

The rest of the lesson passed in a daze, as she stared at her reflection in the mirror and wondered, for the first time in her life, if she was fat. It was all she could think about, this awful new information that she, Mary Jane Watson, was fat.

The first thing she did when she got home from the lesson was to call Wendy.

"Hey, Wendy," she began, suddenly feeling awkward. "Do you think I'm fat?"

Wendy made a snorting noise on the other end. "Do you mean 'phat' with a 'ph,' or 'fat' with an 'f?'"

"With an 'f,'" MJ whispered.

"Puh-leeezze," Wendy pronounced the word with two

42

syllables. "Gimme a break. What happened? Did your mom's creepy boyfriend make another wack comment?"

"Nah. I mean, yeah, he always makes rude comments. But this was from my dance teacher."

"Ruby? That funny old lady with the green eyeshadow?"

"No. Madame Olga. The one with the turban."

"Jeez, MJ. You know how skinny those ballet chicks are. Have you ever been around Lincoln Center when all those little ballerinas with their duck walks and slicked-back hair walk by?"

"Sure," she replied. She didn't want to mention that not too long ago, Mary Jane herself was one of those skinny ballet chicks. Her old dance school was right there.

"Hey, I have an idea," Wendy said excitedly. "Let's get some bubble bath and pour it into the Lincoln Center fountain. Wouldn't that be great? Maybe one of those skinny ballet chicks will fall right on her scrawny butt!"

"Yeah. Sure." Mary Jane swallowed.

So it was true. She was fat.

Well, that was certainly something she could fix. No problem. Her mother was always on a diet, so she knew exactly what to do. All she had to do was cut back a bit.

This was one thing she could fix.

\* \* \*

Miss Ingram stood in front of chemistry class and began her daily attendance call. As usual, Peter Parker was late.

"Okay," Miss Ingram closed her blue attendance notebook. "Today I'm going to pair you off for your science projects. As I've mentioned before..."

Wendy Gonzales' hand shot up, propelling her halfway out of her seat with the force.

"Yes, Wendy?"

"I thought we were allowed to pair up on our own." She cast a swift glance at Mary Jane. "I mean, can't we pick our own partners for the project?"

Miss Ingram shook her head. "Nope. I really think it would be far more productive for me to choose the pairs."

A universal classroom groan was followed by muttered comments, just as the door opened.

"Peter," Miss Ingram said with obvious annoyance, opening her blue book and erasing his absent mark. "Is there any possible way you can make it here on time? Just once, for novelty's sake."

"Sorry, Miss Ingram," he mumbled. "I have Spanish right before this, and it's on the other side of the building way down in the basement and the stairs are always crowded and..."

"Fine, Peter. Just sit down."

"Sorry," he repeated as he walked to his desk. Mary Jane smiled at him, uncertain if he could see her through the stringy hair covering his face.

Poor guy. He seems to go through life apologizing for everything.

"As I was saying," the teacher began again. "I have selected partners for the projects. I have deliberately separated friends, since this is a learning experience, not a social event. Got it? After I read the list of partners, I would like you to quietly—and I mean quietly—get together and discuss possibilities. Remember, this project is deceptively simple: To take a household substance and analyze its chemical elements. Techniques to employ: gas chromatography..."

Someone in the back of the class had muttered something, and a few kids giggled.

"And may I be enlightened as to what is so very humorous?"

There was a brief silence. Finally Harry volunteered. "Um, sorry, Miss Ingram. But one of your students has just suggested we analyze, uh, how should I put it? That we should investigate our own bodily gas after Taco Tuesday in the lunchroom."

Miss Ingram allowed herself a small smile. "Fine I'm glad that's out of the way, the inevitable gas comment. Now we can get on with the project. Okay, here are the partners I've selected."

"This sucks," said Wendy, a little louder than she had intended.

"Miss Gonzales, do you have something to say?"

"No," Wendy flushed. "I just said 'aw, shucks.'"

"Please keep your comments to yourself." Then she began reading the list.

"Sarah Tang and Ben Diaz, Wendy Gonzales and Harry Osborn..."

Suddenly Wendy straightened and shot MJ a wink. Harry Osborn tapped Mary Jane on the shoulder.

"We'll have to pair up for something else," he whispered into her ear. She bit back a shiver.

"...and finally, Mary Jane Watson and Peter Parker."

By the time the last names were read, the class was already buzzing, groups were assembling, and a handful of students had gone to the teacher to complain about their partners.

Mary Jane stood up and walked to the back of the class, where Peter was sitting alone. "Howdy, partner," she said.

He flashed a surprisingly nice smile.

You should smile more, Peter. It looks good on you.

"Howdy," he replied. "This seems vaguely familiar."

She settled into the next desk. "Do you happen to have the remains of Floyd around? Maybe we could just resurrect him. Bring the old bag of bolts back to life and analyze his gas."

"Nothing rises from the dead," he said in a soft voice.

Mary Jane, you idiot! How can you mention the stupid robot when his parents were killed right after that?

"Peter, I'm sorry. I meant..."

Suddenly he grinned. "Hey, let's come up with something fun."

"As opposed to something that's miserable?"

Peter laughed. "How about whatever gives us a good grade?"

They passed the rest of the period going over some ideas, then handed the list to the teacher.

Peter paused as he gathered his books. "So where should we work on this? Your place or mine?"

For a moment she was startled by the light tone in his voice, almost joking. Maybe he wasn't such a geek after all.

Then Harry came up behind him and slapped him on the back, causing his books to fly out of his hands and his glasses to pop off his face.

"Sorry, man," Harry said, handing him back the glasses as MJ helped with the books. "I was just wondering if you have my trig homework."

"Sure, Harry." Peter rifled through a notebook and passed him a two-page worksheet.

"Excellent, bro," Harry winked at Mary Jane. "You even put in some cross-outs so it looks as if I did a little sweating. Thanks. I owe you one."

"You owe me eight," Peter said hesitantly.

"Huh?"

"I've done your homework eight times already."

"Yeah. Right."

Wendy came up and smiled at Harry. "So Harry, should I come by your palace...uh, place this afternoon? We should really jump on this together. I mean, get a jump on this, um, thing."

"Gonzales, I have football practice. Plus we don't know what substance she'll let us do yet."

"Oh, sure," Wendy made a swift cringing face towards MJ.

"See ya," Harry said with another general wink, a lingering look at Mary Jane, and then he left.

"Just kill me now," Wendy moaned.

"Nah," Peter replied, even though Wendy was clearly speaking to MJ. "All you have to do is complete the entire project, make sure you show all of his scary clever work, and hand it in. Just do the whole thing, pull his weight, and you'll probably die of exhaustion anyway."

"That's not nice," Mary Jane said. "I'm sure Harry tries, in his own way."

Peter shrugged. "Yeah, like Harry really has to try. Well, bye."

Then he ambled off.

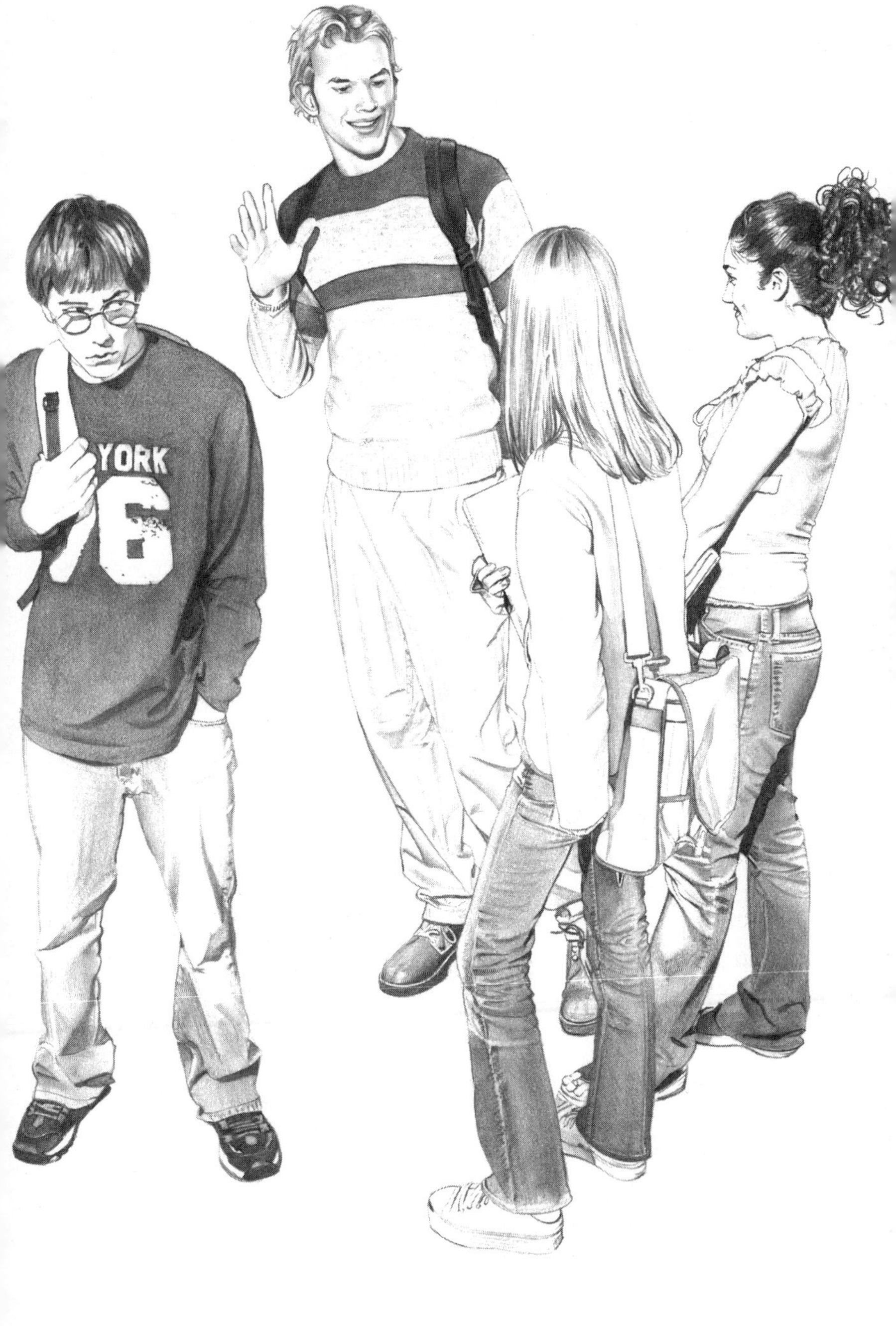
YORK
76

"Can you believe I'm partners with Harry?" Wendy gasped with barely concealed glee. "Harry Osborn! Me and Harry. Mrs. Harry Osborn. Wendy Osborn, rich person. I can see it, can't you?"

"Sure," Mary Jane watched Peter round the corner.

"Really, isn't this cool? I mean, lots of couples get together at first because of science projects. Sorry you got stuck with Peter."

"It's not so bad. Anyway, I wonder how his Aunt May and Uncle Ben are. They must be pretty old by now."

"Uncle Ben?" Wendy laughed. "You mean the rice guy? I'm surprised his aunt isn't Aunt Jemima. And then there are the close family friends, Betty Crocker and Mrs. Paul. Of course you can always count on Duncan Hines in a pinch. And of course there's..."

"Enough! I get your point!"

Wendy kept on with her lame jokes, and Mary Jane pretended to find them funny. But still, she couldn't help but wonder what it would be like to work with Peter Parker after so many years. The Bradford School seemed like a lifetime ago, and in so many ways, for both Peter and Mary Jane, it was.

\* \* \*

Once again, her mother was at a Skye Bleu Party.

Mary Jane crumpled up the note on the refrigerator. This was the third Skye Bleu Party in the past five days, which was good, she supposed. That meant her mom had to haul a bunch of makeup over to some lady's house, chat with everyone at the party, then make them all over using the Skye Bleu Method. In other words, trying to sell the most expensive products to anyone willing to buy.

The other day her mom had gone to a Skye Bleu Party, only to discover a bunch of drunken longshoremen who wanted to be made up. She made a pack of money that night, although MJ didn't really want to hear the details.

So again, she was alone.

There was a dance class in a couple of hours. Might as well take that, even if it was tango night.

Opening the refrigerator door, she looked at the brownish, wilted lettuce, a few carrot sticks, and some bottled water. Almost immediately she closed the door. Why bother to eat if that was the only stuff her mother had around?

Instead she went to the kitchen table and began her homework.

* * *

The big yellow school bus was waiting right in front of the school, ready to take Miss Ingram's science class on a field trip to Osborn Industries.

"This is going to be so cool," Wendy grabbed MJ's arm.

"I hope we get back early. I've got an English test this afternoon."

"God, Watson, give me a break! You're turning into a dork just like Peter Parker."

Mary Jane and Wendy took a seat just over the hump of the rear wheel on the bus as the rest of the class boarded.

"Does this lipstick make me look like a corpse?" Wendy asked after slicking on some frosted pink gloss.

Mary Jane frowned. "I do hope that is a Skye Bleu product."

"But of course. So tell me, do I look dead or what?"

"It's gorgeous. You look spectacular. You'll wow them at Osborn Industries."

"That's my plan," Wendy slipped the tube back in her purse. "What's taking so long?"

"Parker's late again," someone up front said.

"Why don't we just go without him?" Someone else suggested.

Miss Ingram stood by the driver and looked at her watch. "We'll give him another minute or so."

"Here he comes!"

Peter flew out of the front door, then spotted the bus and began to jog towards them with his loping, awkward gait. Panting, he jumped up the bus steps with a sheep-ish smile. "Sorry," he huffed. "My bad."

"Okay. Just find a seat, Peter," Miss Ingram said impatiently.

Mary Jane held her breath, knowing exactly what was coming. And it did.

Slowly he walked down the bus aisle, looking at the occupant of each seat.

"No way, Parker."

"Keep on moving, Monkey Boy."

"Don't even think of sitting here!"

"Peter," Miss Ingram called from the front. "Just sit down! We can't move until you do."

"Sorry," he said again, his eyes behind the glasses pleading.

Mary Jane couldn't stand it. She started to scoot over to make room for him on their seat, but Wendy pushed her back. "Forget it, MJ! There's no room."

He paused for a moment and gave her a weak smile.

Mary Jane suddenly turned to Harry, who was sitting across the aisle by himself. "Hey, Harry," she began in what she hoped was an enticing voice, but soft enough to go unheard by most of the bus.

Harry immediately straightened. "Hello, Mary Jane."

"Can you do me a favor?"

"Sure!"

"Can you let Peter sit with you?"

"Well..."

"As I remember, you said the other day you owe him one. I would be so disappointed to find out you're not a man of your word."

Immediately Harry moved his jacket aside. "Come on here, buddy," he said to Peter, leaning over to see Mary Jane's reaction. But she was already looking at Peter.

"Thanks," he said as he brushed past her. His face was red, his gaze downcast.

Did I make a mistake?

The bus started rolling, and she looked over at Peter a few times. Harry was talking to him, and he nodded, shrugged, and gave the usual Parker responses.

Within forty-five minutes they pulled onto the grounds of Osborn Industries. And even Wendy grew silent.

"Oh," she breathed. "I had no idea."

Apparently no one did. The entire busload stared in wide-eyed amazement at the lavish acres of green lawn and expertly maintained hedges, all leading up to the glass-domed colossus with Osborn Industries stamped on top.

"Wow," Wendy finally said.

Mary Jane turned back to Harry, and for the first time he seemed uncomfortable.

"Hey, Harry," someone yelled from the back seat. "Can I borrow a grand?"

Everyone laughed nervously, and Harry replied.

"Sure." He seemed to be thinking of a comeback, and Mary Jane saw Peter lean over and say something. Harry suddenly brightened. "Sure! *The Daily Bugle* is offering two thousand bucks for proof of alien life. Turn yourself in, and we'll split it."

It wasn't funny. In fact, it was pretty stupid, but it relieved the weird tension, and the bus returned to normal.

So, Harry. Once again, you owe one to Peter.

The first half of the field trip was not that exciting. They walked through long corridors with shiny marble floors, saw a bunch of busy-looking people in white jackets with clipboards. Mary Jane kept on wondering what was actually produced at Osborn Industries, but no one seemed able to give a concise answer.

Then they were led to a room with a slick blue Consumer Products Development sign over the door. Inside, the room was very modern, with long tables set up with little paper cups filled with bright blue, green, orange, red and yellow liquids.

"Don't tell me we have to pee in those cups?" Wendy whispered.

"Or worse," Mary Jane replied. "Someone already has!"

There was a commotion, and a tall man with high cheekbones and strange eyes entered the room. The white-coated clipboard people all stood out of the way to allow him to pass.

"Hello, kiddies," he said in a surprisingly soft voice.

Everyone had to be silent, to lean forward to catch the words. "I am Norman Osborn."

That was Harry's dad! Mary Jane automatically whirled around to look at Harry, who was busy looking down at his jacket cuffs. There was only a slight resemblance.

"I have quite a treat for you kids." Norman Osborn did not even look at his son. "Before you, in these colorful little cups, is the latest in hydration technology. We call it..." With a theatrical flourish, he raised his right arm and pointed to a blue velvet curtain. Instantaneously, the curtain opened, revealing a huge sign in block letters.

"OZ!" Osborn announced. And the clipboard people all began to clap, sliding the clipboards under their arms. Slowly, the kids clapped, too, more because they couldn't think of any other response.

"Go ahead, kiddies. Drink up!"

"What's in it?" A single voice asked.

"Everything designed to make you all the best you can be. There's taurine, ginseng, glucosamine, ginko biloba, electrolytes..." His gaze darted around the room, lighting for a moment on Mary Jane. A weird feeling went up her spine, not frightening. She couldn't place it.

It's his eyes! They look almost reptilian.

Slowly, one by one at first, with a little hesitation, the kids stepped up to the cups and sipped.

"Hey, this stuff is good!"

"Not bad. Sort of like a sports drink, but better."

"Cool! It makes your tongue orange!"

Mary Jane just watched Mr. Osborn. He whispered to some of the clipboard people, and walked around with his hands clasped behind his back. It wasn't that he was ugly, or mean. He was almost handsome, in an oily kind of way. He was clearly a man of great power. Yet he seemed a little cold, perhaps. Driven. Intense.

After a few minutes he cleared his throat. "How did you like it?"

Everyone applauded, nodding with approval. Miss Ingram was staring at Mr. Osborn with an expression that seemed to invite more than the usual parent-teacher conference.

"I have more good news, kiddies. Your very own high school will be the first test audience of OZ. I have reached an agreement with the school board. And after the drink is tested, after our patent is granted, you will also have the very first new gymnasium built by OZ! A healthy place for healthy bodies!"

Now everyone was clapping wildly, except for Harry, Mary Jane and Peter, who just looked at her and shrugged.

"This is a little weird," Peter shook his head. "A pep rally for some new sports drink."

Mr. Osborn personally saw to it that every cup was drained before he would leave the room.

The next stop on the tour was a massive round lab with "Development Room" on the doublewide doors. It was like something out of a science fiction flick, with an electron microscope, canisters labeled with biohazard signs, and multiple computer workstations with huge, flat-panel screens.

"Cool," Peter said.

They had lagged behind, and Peter was staring at the labels on cages with white mice. "Look, Mary Jane. This one's for a testosterone formula."

"For or against it?" She asked.

He chuckled. "Hard to tell. The mice look pretty butch, though."

"What's that?" She pointed to another bank of cages.

"I don't know. Spiders—South American, I think. The one with the red stripes is pretty rare."

"It's kind of pretty."

"Funny, they probably think we're pretty disgusting. Hey, look at that one!"

"Come on, Peter. We're falling behind."

"No, really! Come here and...OUCH!"

"What happened?"

Peter held out his right hand. Already the back was beginning to puff up and turn red. "I think I got bitten." He fell against a glass cage filled with more spiders.

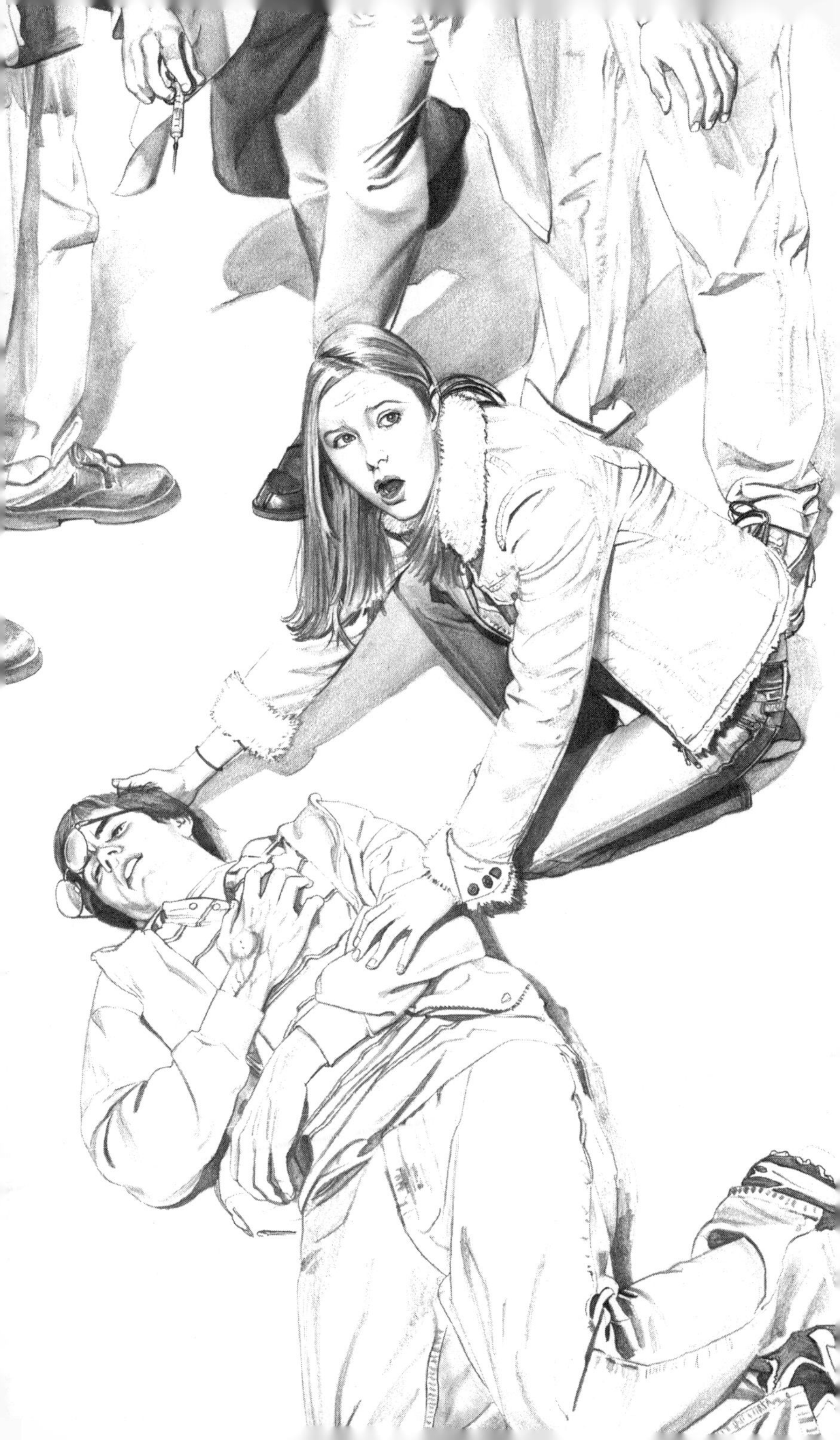

"Miss Ingram!" Mary Jane called. "Miss Ingram! Peter's been hurt!"

"No, Mary...I..."

She rushed to his side, just in time to see his eyes roll back, and then he slammed to the floor.

"My God!" Miss Ingram turned to the woman who had been leading the tour. "Can anyone help?"

At once it seemed as if white-coated employees materialized out of nowhere. The kids all stood back and watched with detached interest.

Mary Jane took off her jean jacket, balled it up and slipped it under his head. "Peter? Peter, it's me. Please wake up."

Then his eyes opened slowly. "What happened?"

"I think a rare South American spider tried to eat you."

"Cool." He sat up unsteadily, aided by white jackets, Miss Ingram and Mary Jane. Still pale, he was helped to his feet.

"Are you all right, Peter?" Miss Ingram asked with a combination of concern and annoyance.

Sure. Now that you know he won't kick during your field trip, you're ticked that he's caused a scene that might get back to Mr. Osborn. Nice taste in men, lady.

"Yeah, I'm fine."

The rest of the class was ordered back to the bus, and Miss Ingram made him promise to see the nurse once they returned to school.

"That really looks as if it hurts," Mary Jane said as they walked across the parking lot.

"It does. Feels like a really big wasp sting."

"I've never been stung by a wasp."

"Sure you have. Don't you remember all those years at the Bradford School?"

It took her a moment to realize he had just made a joke. "Very funny."

"Hey, Mary Jane? You coming or what?" Wendy called from ahead.

"I think I'll sit with Peter on the way back." Then she looked at him. "Is that okay?"

He shrugged, still looking at his hand.

"Why don't you sit with Harry?" She suggested to Wendy.

"Great idea! I saw a few spots inside that could use a potted plant or two. I'll suggest some decorating ideas."

They filed into the bus, Miss Ingram took a head count, and soon they were on their way back to the school.

"Thank you, MJ," Peter said.

"For what?"

Their faces were only inches apart, and she was startled to realize that his eyes weren't bad. Up close, behind the glasses, they were actually nice. Beautiful, in fact. They were blue with little flecks of green. Funny, she hadn't noticed that before.

"Thank you for being such a good friend," he said.

Her stomach did a peculiar flip, and for a long moment she just stared at him. There was something in those eyes, something deep and wonderful.

And suddenly, she wanted him to kiss her. Badly. Right there on the bus.

"Mary Jane, I…"

That's when the apple core hit his head.

"Ha! Parker got attacked by a spider!"

"Class, calm down," Miss Ingram yelled, but she had a slight smile on her face.

Mary Jane looked back at Peter, who sat with his head down and his cheeks flushed.

What was I thinking? I wanted HIM to kiss me? As if!

She, too, grinned, not seeing Peter's expression as he glanced at her.

"Don't forget to see the school nurse," she said as she threw her jacket over her shoulder and left the bus with Wendy.

"Sure," he said to himself.

But instead he went straight home, past Aunt May and Uncle Ben in the kitchen, and right up to bed. His hand throbbing, all he could think of was that little grin on her face.

\* \* \*

Her mother and Mike were in the living room when she came back from school.

"Hi, Mom."

"Hello, honey. Aren't you going to say anything to Mike?"

Sure. How about a nice bowl of rat poison, Mike?

"Hello, Mike." She was unable to keep the sarcasm from her voice.

How could her mother spend time with such a jerk?

"Now, sweetie pie, you can do better than that," Mike called.

Yeah, so can my mom.

"I'm going over to dance class. See you later," she said, grabbing her ballet bag.

"Honey, why don't you skip it tonight? Mike here made a special effort to have dinner with both of us."

"I'm not really hungry."

"Mary Jane, you haven't had a decent meal in days. Skip ballet and have some pizza. Or would you rather have take-out from that Chinese place? You know, the one with all the cute red lanterns."

"Forget it, Mom. I really need to get to ballet."

"Don't talk to your mother like that," Mike growled.

"You're not my dad, Mike," she said.

"What did you say?" She could hear him get off the couch.

"Mike, honey. Just let her go off to ballet."

"Well, he's not, is he?" MJ asked, suddenly furious.

"She needs discipline. That's what she needs."

"No, please, Mike. Leave her alone."

Something in her mother's voice made a chill run through her. Without thinking any further, she rushed past Mike, elbowing him in the side, and ran out the door clutching her ballet bag.

"Why you little bitch!" His voice was harsh, cruel— a tone she had never heard before.

"Mike! Stop!" Her mother cried.

He started to go after her, but she ran faster, knowing he could never catch up to her. She ran for blocks, it seemed, putting as much distance between herself and the apartment as she possibly could. At a corner phone booth she called Wendy, and asked if she could spend the night there.

"Sure," Wendy said. "Oh, my mom says come over now for dinner."

"Thanks, but I've already eaten. I have ballet class and stuff."

"Anything wrong?"

"Nah," she lied. "My mom has a couple of Skye Bleu parties, and she didn't want me to be alone. Thanks, Wendy! I'll see you in a few hours."

Wendy started to say something, but Mary Jane simply hung up. For some reason she did want to speak to someone. Needed to speak to someone. Biting her lip, she put the quarter into the slot and dialed Peter's number.

"Hello?" It was Aunt May.

"Hi. This is Mary Jane. Mary Jane Watson. You probably don't remember me, but..."

"Why of course I do, dear! How are you? Peter is so delighted you two are once again at the same school. How's your mother doing?"

"Oh, she's fine, thank you." There was a lump in her throat, and it was hard for her to speak. "Is Peter there?"

"Yes, dear, he is. But I'm afraid he's not feeling well. He came straight home from school and went to his room. Shall I wake him for you?"

"No, no thank you. I'll see him at school tomorrow. And it was nice speaking to you again."

"You too, Mary Jane. And I'll tell him you called."

She hung up the receiver and stared at the still, silent phone for a few moments. Then she slung her ballet bag over her back and jogged over to class. With a little luck, she could do three lessons back-to-back.

With a little luck, she wouldn't have the energy to think.

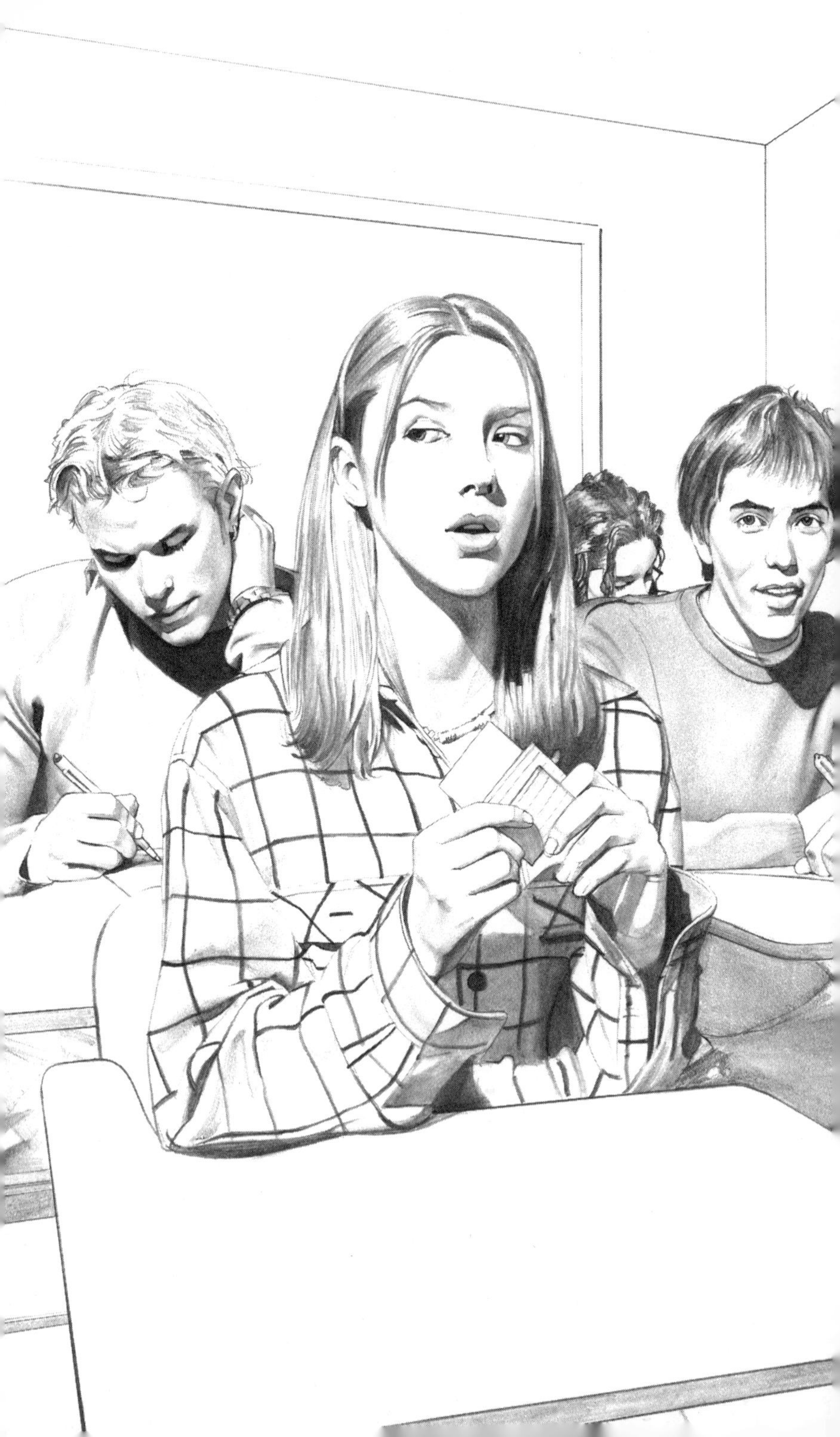

# chapter 3

Miss Ingram, as usual, stood at the head of the class with her constant companion, the blue attendance booklet. With a smart, authoritative snap she closed the leaves and turned to the blackboard, chalk poised.

"Okay, class. Before we discuss the projects, I want you all to write at least a full page—single spaced, no large printing—on three specific scientific facts you learned yesterday at Osborn Industries. These can be anything that struck you, from..."

The door opened, and the late-straggler entered, books piled in arms, head cast down.

"Miss Watson," the teacher said with a blandness that masked her surprise, putting down her chalk. "You are late."

"I'm sorry," she said softly.

As Mary Jane navigated the narrow aisle to her seat, she was aware of the eyes focused on her from all sides.

Yeah, like I'm the only one here who has ever been late to a class?

Glancing up, she saw a startling sight. There, comfortable at his desk, with all the ease of a corporate executive, was Peter Parker. He grinned and winked at her. It took her a few seconds to realize the shock value of what she could actually see: His eyes. Not only was his hair pushed off his forehead, but also he wasn't wearing those Coke-bottle glasses.

She stumbled, dropping a book. Without hesitation, Peter bounded to her side, replaced the book, and returned neatly to his place.

"Mary Jane, could you please sit down?" Miss Ingram sighed.

"Oh, sure. Sorry."

She slid into her chair, resisting the urge to turn around and simply stare at Peter. How had he moved so fast to pick up her books and return to his seat? And how had he managed to get to class so early?

Suddenly, strangely, she felt unkempt, uncomfortable. Although she had spent the night at Wendy's, and her parents had been incredibly kind, she felt as if she had just camped out for a week.

Sleep had eluded her, even on the snug sofa bed. Today she wore her own jeans, paired with one of Wendy's shirts. While it suited her friend perfectly, it just didn't feel right on MJ. Perhaps it was the style, a flame-red flannel button-down, like something an Alaskan lumberjack would wear.

Harry Osborn snorted, then pressed his pencil eraser tip into her shoulder. "Slick threads, Watson."

She didn't bother to respond.

The teacher continued speaking, as Mary Jane wondered if her mother was furious with her. Or if she hadn't even noticed she was gone. That was the more likely scenario. Wendy sat across the room, tapping a pen against her lip. Another kid was reading the latest *Sports Illustrated* on his lap.

Then everything was quiet, and she realized that the other students were all busy writing. What were they writing? What had she missed?

Something hit her lightly on the shoulder. At first she assumed it was Harry, but she turned around anyway. Harry was also busy writing, a look of pained concentration on his face, his tongue jutting from the side of his mouth. She looked down, and found a small piece of paper folded into a triangle. As discreetly as possible, she picked it up and unfolded it.

*Hey, MJ. Looking a little sleepy there! The assignment is to write a full page, no double spacing allowed, on three scientific facts you observed on yesterday's field trip. May I suggest the velocity of an apple core when hurled at someone's head on a moving bus? Good luck. PP*

She blinked and re-read the note, and smiled, giving him a small thumb's-up sign from beneath her desk.

After class Peter lightly brushed her arm. "Are you okay? Aunt May said you called last night."

"Yeah, sorry about that. I just wanted, um, to see

how you were feeling after the spider bite and everything."

"Oh, thanks. I'm feeling fine. Great, in fact. Guess I just needed more sleep than usual. Slept straight through dinner and everything." Then he paused. "What else is up?"

"Well, maybe we should start working on the project. And I hate to say this, but it might be hard to work at my house. It's just that..."

"Things are a little tense there." He spoke calmly, a simple statement of fact.

"Yes. Sort of. How did you know?"

"That's Wendy's shirt. I've noticed it before because I used to have one just like it in sixth grade, no offense. Sears boys' department. And you look tired, again, no offense. So I can only assume you spent an unplanned night over at Wendy's."

"Wow, that's amazing! You really got all that from my shirt?"

"Yeah, that and the fact that Wendy blabbed to everyone before class that you'd spent the night after a major blow-out with your mom."

She laughed, surprised that she still had an ounce of laughter in her. Then he grew more serious. "Listen, MJ. Why don't you just come straight over to my place after school, and we can start work on the project? Aunt May would be forever grateful if you'd have dinner with us. Seems Uncle Ben and I don't compliment her enough on her cooking, so a fresh audience would be appreciated by everyone. Then I can drop you off at home as late as you want, hopefully after your mom's already asleep. That would give you a good night's rest in your own bed. Plus it might be easier to face the world with the use of your own toothbrush."

Immediately she clamped a hand over her mouth.

Does my breath smell skanky?

"I have ballet class tonight. I really have to go." Her voice was muffled.

"Then come over after ballet. We'll still be able to get a few hours of work done, and you'll still be able to praise Aunt May on her organic vegetable medley."

She was about to say maybe, that it sounded like a good idea, and by the way, did you get contact lenses? But before she could form an answer he looked up at the clock.

"Whoops. Gotta run to gym. See ya later, MJ." He took a few jogging steps forward, then, over his shoulder, shouted, "And I can't figure it out either. I just woke up and could see without them. Bye."

"Bye," she mouthed before adding, "Weird."

* * *

71

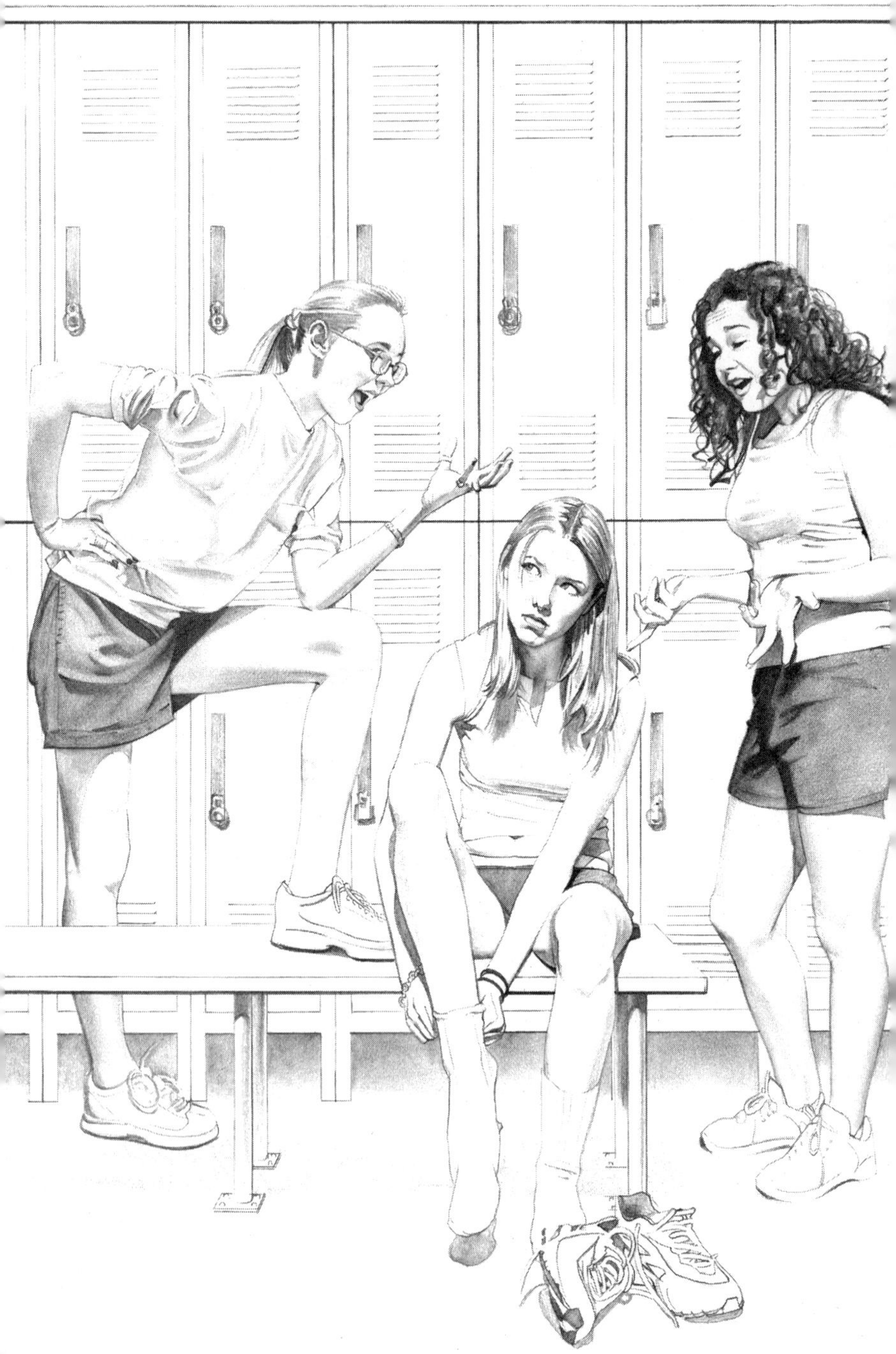

It was the talk of the school.

By final period, all anyone could discuss was what had happened in third-period gym class with Peter Parker and Flash Thompson, the senior basketball phenom.

"Did you hear?" Wendy burst breathlessly when she caught up with Mary Jane in the girls' locker room.

"Hear what?" MJ leaned her forehead against her locker, dialing the combination.

"About Peter. Peter Parker."

For an instant Mary Jane felt her stomach drop. "Oh my God, is he okay?"

"Yeah, he's fine. It's Flash Thompson who's a mess."

"Flash Thompson? What does Flash Thompson have to do with Peter?"

"Okay, well, you know how Flash loves to razz Peter. Calls him names, you know, stuff like Pee-Pee Parker, and Pansy Parker. Real mature names like that."

"Sure," she smiled, remembering Pukey Parker from grade school. "Children can be so cruel."

"So in gym class Flash yells something, I don't remember what."

"It was 'Slowpoke Parker,'" stated Alison Myers from two lockers down. "He called him Slowpoke right before they started doing laps around the gym to warm up for a basketball scrimmage."

"Right," Wendy nodded, slightly annoyed at her story being hijacked. "Anyway, so..."

"So Flash yells Slowpoke, and next thing everyone knows, Parker has run around the gym twice! I'm not kidding! No one could believe it—he was just this human bullet!"

"Hey, I was telling the story!" Wendy straightened, her eyes narrowing at Alison, who promptly shut up.

"Sorry," she retorted, flipping her hair.

"So, as I was saying, Peter passes everyone not once, but twice! Coach Renny almost had a stroke. You know how he adores Flash, and lets him pick on Peter as much as he wants. Actually, Coach Renny picks on Peter all the time himself."

"I didn't know that," Mary Jane closed her locker. "That sucks."

"Well, so Coach Renny and Flash are, like, in total shock. Flash is convinced it was all some trick, or an optical illusion. So he challenges Peter to a race—just the two of them."

"In the middle of gym class? And Coach Renny let him get away with it?"

"Of course he did," Alison chirped. "Everyone knows he loves Flash and hates Peter!"

"Myers, could you please let me tell it?"

"Sorry, Wendy," she replied without any remorse.

"What happened?" Mary Jane asked.

"Coach stops the whole class and sets up a race. Not really a race, more of an obstacle course. Like something from friggin' boot camp. All of the other guys are practically peeing in their shorts, hoping they don't have to join in. But they don't. Coach is out to humiliate Parker. So he sets up this little course with a bunch of hurdles, a two-mile run, ending with both guys having to climb up ropes to the ceiling."

"Not the ropes!"

"Don't forget the long jump part," Alison added. "Between the hurdle and the ropes, they have to do the long jump. Can you imagine?"

"So Flash is beginning to get worried, sweating a little. I mean, even for Flash Thompson this is pretty extreme. But Peter..."

"Peter is calm as a cucumber," Alison interjected. Wendy glared at her. "Well, he was! My boyfriend is in that class."

"Right," Wendy snapped. "So Peter is as cool as a cucumber. Cool, not calm. Vegetables cannot be calm, Myers. Anyway, Coach Renny blows his little whistle and the race is on. But not for long."

"Oh, no. Poor Peter."

"Not Poor Peter. It's Poor Flash. Peter Parker zoomed through the whole thing in double-time. He sat there waiting for Flash to finish, which he never did because he started crying by the time he got to the rope."

"He started crying?"

"Yup."

"What did Peter do then?"

"He walked over to the hoops and started shooting baskets!" Alison clapped. "Coach yelled at Peter, of course. Said he had an attitude problem and made him do laps the rest of gym period, but everyone was pretty stunned. Especially Coach Renny and Flash. Peter never even worked up a sweat. It was really weird."

Weird. That's exactly what it is, weird.

"Wow," was all Mary Jane could think to say. "Wow."

"Yeah, so now Coach wants to recruit Peter for the basketball team," Wendy concluded.

"But Flash is the star of the team!"

"Flash used to be the star of the team," Alison corrected. "I have a feeling Parker's about to elbow in on some of that glory."

"You know him pretty well, Mary Jane. What's he like?"

"Peter?"

"No. Coach Renny," Wendy sighed. "Of course I mean Peter Parker! What's he like?"

"Well, he's very nice," she answered uncertainly. "He's always been very nice."

"You know, I was looking at him this afternoon, and he's actually pretty cute," Alison clutched her books to her chest in a strangely flirtatious way, as if the object of their discussion could actually see her. "I've always thought so. He has beautiful eyes. Has he always had beautiful eyes?"

"I guess so," Mary Jane shrugged.

"You are so lucky to have him for a science project partner. I mean, Harry Osborn is okay. But Peter is really cool. Plus, he's so much smarter than Harry. I have a feeling I'm going to have to pull Harry's considerable dead weight. With Peter, it's pretty much an automatic 'A.'"

"Yeah, well. I've got to get to ballet class now."

"Are you spending the night at my house again?" Wendy asked. "You're more than welcome. My parents think you're a much better kid than I am. I suspect they're angling for a switch-a-roo of sorts."

"Oh, no thanks, Wendy. I think I'll brave my own mom tonight. But thanks anyway."

"You're welcome. And no rush in returning the shirt. I kind of like seeing what it looks like when covering actual boobs. Still waiting for mine to come in, so seeing you in my shirt is the closest I'll get to that for a while. Catch ya later, MJ."

"Bye-bye," waved Alison.

Both Alison and Wendy left together, elbow to elbow, chattering about Peter, how cute he was, how clever and funny and all-around spectacular. Mary Jane stood at her closed locker for a few moments, ballet bag in hand, feeling unsettled and trying to imagine Peter as some sort of athletic whiz-kid, a romantic heartbreaker.

Peter Parker, Teen Idol. Popular Peter Parker. Prince Peter. Peter Parker, Passionate Paramour...

From the corner of her eye she saw someone walk by the girls' locker room with the principal. She quickly leaned out the door to see Mr. Osborn turn the corner, laughing, making a sweeping gesture towards the gym.

"Weird," she said at last.

\* \* \*

Stepping into the Parker household was like entering a time-warp. Everything was just as Mary Jane had remembered it almost a decade earlier, even the rather scruffy bushes out front and the porch swing with faded floral cushions tied to the seat.

"Why, Mary Jane Watson!" Aunt May exclaimed, her hands framing her cheeks in a look of surprise. "Peter mentioned how lovely you've become, but really, he failed to do you justice. Please come in, my dear."

She flushed at the compliment and stepped inside, where the time-warp effect was even more pronounced. The furniture was the same, from the long brown sofa with rough, nubby upholstery to the green footstool. There was a coffee table with one of the legs still bent at a precarious angle.

How could it have remained upright for so long?

The paintings on the wall were done by Peter's mother, some when she was an art student, such as the quirky landscape featuring a purple cow, or the flower vase filled with blossoms made of bright yellow peace signs. There were a few she had done of Peter as a baby, and one that must have been completed just before she died, of Peter in his Bradford tie and blazer.

Now there were newer photographs as well, not replacing the older ones, just tucked beside them. There were family pictures of Peter with his aunt and uncle. In each picture Peter was taller, his aunt and uncle, grayer. They looked like the type of pictures taken in a department store or at a mall, with a fake library backdrop, the sort of picture you get taken once a year with the twenty-five dollar coupon from the Sunday paper.

Mary Jane found the pictures inexplicably moving.

The sounds of ascending footsteps rattled the house as Peter emerged from the basement, the door suddenly bursting open.

"Hey, MJ," he took her ballet bag and backpack, and with a casual grace threw them both over his left shoulder. "This is my Aunt May."

"We've already had a nice chat, haven't we, Mary Jane?"

"Yes, ma'am," she replied. She hadn't used "ma'am" in years, but somehow it seemed appropriate with Aunt May.

Peter rolled his eyes with obvious affection, and Aunt May swatted him with a dishtowel.

"So how was Ruby's House-O-Dance today?"

"Um, fine, it was tap, tango and gymnastics."

She blinked as she spoke, startled for two reasons. First, she couldn't remember telling him where she took classes. And secondly, his smile was almost blindingly white.

Hadn't he worn braces just the other day, big, thick ones with multi-colored rubber bands? Or was he one of those kids who just always seemed to wear braces?

"Oh, Mary Jane, you must be famished! All that dancing," Aunt May said with a click of her tongue. "I made tuna casserole for dinner, his mother's recipe. Peter mentioned you enjoyed it so as a child." Her whispy white hair was fastened in the back with a large tortoise shell clip, and her features were delicate and lovely, with a fine-lined complexion and distinct laugh lines bracketing her mouth. As she spoke she began to untie her apron, then she held up her hands in defeat and turned to Peter, who untied the bow with the flick of one hand. "I just popped the casserole into the oven, and there are snacks in the fridge in case you two can't wait."

"Actually, I'm not really hungry," Mary Jane began. But Aunt May didn't seem to take notice.

"So you kids get started on the project. Be brilliant." She folded the apron neatly and tossed it on a chair. "Meanwhile, I'll be right where I belong, playing poker on the Internet." With that, she walked towards a computer with a garish "Viva Las Vegas!" twirling on the screen.

"Aunt May's got quite the gambling streak," Peter laughed. Then he held the basement door open. "To the laboratory," he said in a thick Transylvanian accent. "After you."

She hesitated, and he shrugged and jumped ahead of her, taking the stairs two at a time and the bottom four in one giant leap.

"Peter, careful!" She followed behind, but stopped midway down the staircase.

If the rest of the house had changed very little, the basement was a virtual time capsule. He watched her face as she descended the steps.

"My God, Peter! It's exactly as it was when we worked on the last project together."

He put down her ballet bag and backpack, then flipped over the freestanding blackboard. There, in the corner, was the small drawing Peter's dad had sketched of Floyd the robot, complete with the flowers she drew with colored chalk at his roller-feet.

"You always wanted to make things prettier, nicer," Peter said softly.

She glanced up at him, his eyes incredibly blue and intense, almost mesmerizing.

Then he flipped the blackboard back to the other side. It was covered with chalk notations, formulas and dots where his father had clearly paused to think, followed by more notations written with haste and excitement.

"What's this?" Then the scribbling began to make sense. "Your father's work."

"Yeah. Wish I knew what it was. Might make us all rich if I could finish my dad's formula."

"Peter," she stepped closer, almost touching the blackboard, near enough to erase the precious, long-ago, fragile marks with a single touch, a whispered breath.

He said nothing, not ordering her back, not telling her to watch out. Instead he just observed her.

"Any idea what this is a formula for?"

He shrugged. "I don't know exactly. They were very excited about it, and were presenting the preliminary findings in Switzerland."

"Do you have a copy of those findings?"

He shoved his hands into his jean pockets. "Nope. They had the papers with them when they, uh, when they died."

"Peter, I'm sorry..."

"So am I," he overlapped with a cheerful bounce on his heels. "If they'd only had enough foresight and consideration to leave a copy behind, we'd ace this project for sure."

"That's not what I meant."

He swallowed, then looked directly at her. "I know."

She glanced away.

"Hey, MJ," he said gently. "I've been meaning to ask...I mean. Have you ever heard from your father?"

She shook her head. "No. Not directly. I know he's alive someplace. Granny Watson hears from him now and then."

"I...I wonder what's worse. Knowing you'll never have a father again, or wondering if he'll ever come back."

"I know my father's not coming back."

He nodded. "I guess, then, we both know. About our fathers, I mean."

Something passed between them, an understanding. For a long moment they simply stared at each other. He spoke first. "Mary Jane, I...damn! What the hell?"

"What's wrong?"

"My hands are stuck. Look, I can't pull them out of my pockets without taking the whole insides. Crap!"

"You must have gum in there or something," she said, even as she could see there was no gum. Yet his hands were absolutely fixed to the pockets. Finally, after struggling and yanking and, lastly, laughing as they pulled together, his hands were free.

"Gotta confess," she shook her head. "I don't ever want to know what was in there!"

"Must be some of Aunt May's organic detergent gone amok." He glanced up with an amused smirk.

"Speaking of going amok, what happened in gym class today? God, Peter, the whole school's talking about it."

His face reddened. "I don't know," he examined his hands. "Damn, this stuff is sticky. Anyway, I just got sick of Flash ragging on me all the time. I've always sort of taken it, just sucked it up. But between Flash and Coach Renny, I just couldn't take it anymore."

"Did you really do all that stuff they're saying? I mean, the ropes and hurdles and then the baskets?"

"Yeah," then he looked directly at her, almost slipping his hands back into his pockets until he stopped himself. "It was the strangest thing, but I knew—and I mean knew—I could beat his ass. And I did. Hey, nobody was more surprised than I was, not really."

"Have you ever done any of that stuff before?"

"Nah. But then, I've never tried." He went to the foot of the basement steps to make sure the door was closed. Satisfied that no one else could hear them, he returned. "Okay, now this is going to sound weird," he began.

"Okay," she encouraged. "Go on."

"I think something happened when that spider bit me on the field trip."

"Duh. You passed out."

"No, after that. Later, during the night. I mean, this morning I woke up and for the first time since I can even remember, I didn't reach for my glasses. I mean, usually it takes me twenty minutes to even find them, that's how blind I am. But I jumped out of bed and forgot about them until I stepped on them."

"You stepped on them? Are they broken?"

"Totally pulverized. So I freaked out, realizing this would be the second pair Aunt May and Uncle Ben would have to buy me this month. I mean, after last week, when Flash threw the football at my face and broke the other ones."

"Oh, yeah. I forgot about that."

"Well, so I freaked out. All I could imagine was the

massive safety glasses they said I would have to get next time. These things look like goggles, for Christ's sake, with a big black elastic band around my head. I'm thinking, things couldn't get much worse. But then I stopped. I could see! I mean, really, really see without them. I looked out the window and could see individual leaves on the trees, the cracks on the driveway. I could read the brand name of a crumpled gum wrapper from a half block away. I saw Rochelle Silverman down the street walking her dog. And you know what?"

"What?"

"She's not that hot after all. Her skin is nasty, and she had all this orange make-up all over it. And I'm pretty sure she has a mustache."

"Really? I didn't know about the mustache. Anyway, maybe your eyes have improved," she suggested. "Remember that kid in third grade? The one who always had a patch over one eye."

"You mean Lazy-Eye Larry?"

"That's the one. Seems all he had were weak eyes, and they got stronger on their own. Maybe you haven't really needed your glasses for a while, you just never knew it."

"That thought crossed my mind as well," he admitted. "But then things got even weirder."

"Yeah?"

"Mary Jane," he seemed uncertain of how to continue. "MJ, um, I have a six pack."

She knew this required some sort of serious response. It seemed so important to him. "Okay," she said earnestly. "Is it stashed under your bed or something?"

"Huh?"

"The beer. Is it hidden someplace?"

"Not beer. Um, this."

Very slowly he lifted up his shirt.

"Peter, what are you...holy!"

Buff wasn't the word. Ripped was a little closer, but still not quite accurate to describe the torso he just revealed. It was like something out of a comic book, some giant warrior beast from another planet. Or a kids' action figure. Every muscle was huge, defined as if it had been drawn for an anatomy textbook on the uber-male.

"Jeez, Peter," she gasped. "You're embossed! Can I touch it?"

"Yeah, sure. Go ahead."

Gingerly she stepped towards him, and ran her fingertips over his abdomen. It was almost unreal, inhuman, hard as if made of something other than mere flesh. He was honed.

Yet it was also warm, soft.

Wow.

With a sharp intake of breath he dropped the shirt back.

"Uh, see what I mean?" He didn't tuck the shirt back in, and seemed flustered.

"Maybe you worked out in your sleep?" she

suggested lamely, still rattled by the sight—and feel—of his body.

"Sure. Happens all the time. Scrawny kid falls asleep looking like a scarecrow, and wakes up the next morning, well. Like this."

"Your arms look bigger, too," she said with wonder. "I noticed that before. May I?" She reached out to touch his biceps, and after only a slight hesitation, he nodded.

They, too, were nothing short of spectacular—hard, solid, strong, knotted.

Wow!

"Peter, how on earth did..." The words faded into oblivion.

They were so close she could feel the heat from his body.

"Mary Jane," his voice was husky. And slowly, his hand reached up to her shoulder. She could feel him touch her as his hand skimmed over the fabric of the shirt she'd changed into after ballet.

Then the basement door flew open.

"Hey, kiddies!" Aunt May shouted from the top of the steps. "Dinner's ready!"

Peter jumped back—across the room in a single hop.

Taking half her blouse with him.

"Oh, no!" He stared at Mary Jane in her ripped shirt, her white bra with the little pink bow visible.

"Peter!" She felt like her entire body was glowing red with embarrassment as she attempted to cover herself. Yet even through her shock, she realized her shirt was still stuck on his fingers, as if he'd soaked his hands in Perma-Glue.

"I'm so sorry, MJ! I mean, I don't know how this happened," he struggled with the cloth, bunching it from hand to hand.

"What's going on?" She could barely breathe.

"I don't know." His voice was raw with honesty.

Thinking quickly, she reached for her bag, which still contained Wendy's loathsome red shirt. She slipped it on, then helped Peter tug off the shredded remains of her new blouse from his sticky hands.

"I didn't mean... what I mean," he shook his head.

"I know." She buttoned the shirt up as he still stared at his hands.

After a few moments of hormonally addled confusion, Peter cleared his throat. "Dinner," his voice cracked.

"Yeah." Then she smiled. "Well..."

He closed his eyes, shook his head, then opened them again, this time his gaze clear and focused. "So," he said in a stronger tone. "The sticky stuff on my hands. Everything else. The only answer I can come up with is the spider bite. What do you think happened to me?"

Who cares about you! What just happened to ME?!

"Um, I don't know. I really don't have any idea. But I do know one thing, Peter."

"Yeah?"

"It ain't all bad."

A slow grin spread across his face. "It doesn't totally suck," he admitted. "But about your shirt..."

"It doesn't matter." And it was true. It didn't really matter.

"Kiddies! Come on up!" Aunt May yelled a second time.

Mary Jane stopped. "Peter!"

"Yeah?"

Her mind was spinning. Aunt May's shout of "kiddies" reminded her of Norman Osborn...of the field trip...of...

"OZ!"

"Huh?"

"What happened to you, this new buff Peter. And that drink, OZ, with the ingredients..."

"Why didn't I think of that before? Of course!"

"Hey," she grabbed his arm. "Let's analyze OZ for our project!"

"Where will we get it?"

"We're supposed to have it in gym classes by Friday."

"Mary Jane, you're brilliant!"

With that they went upstairs. But something had changed, as if there was some invisible electric charge between the two of them.

They entered the kitchen, both with flushed faces and overly bright eyes.

"Looks as if the two of you got down to some serious work down there," Aunt May said after one look at them. "Why, Mary Jane. You're even wearing a work shirt." Then she squinted. "Are your buttons misbuttoned?"

"Oh," she immediately fumbled with the shirt.

"Yep," Peter answered with crisp deliberation. "Got lots accomplished."

Uncle Ben was at the sink washing up.

"Good. I'll bet you two make a great team," he said over his shoulder. Then he dried his hands and walked over to Mary Jane.

"Mary Jane, how pretty you are," he smiled warmly. He was wearing a pair of overalls and a flannel shirt— not unlike the one she was wearing. He looked much older than he did at the Parkers' funeral, but of course that was a long time ago. "You've become a beautiful young woman." Then he chuckled. "And yes, you're right. I'm old as hell. I swear, May, don't you think we're aging in dog years?"

"Speak for yourself." She placed the casserole on a potholder in the center of the table. "And no, Peter, you will not avoid my vegetable medley tonight."

"Vegetable muddle," he hissed to Mary Jane.

"I heard that." Aunt May poured iced tea from a pitcher painted with roosters.

"You have to watch out for May," Uncle Ben said as he held his wife's chair. Peter held Mary Jane's carefully, using his wrist so his fingers wouldn't stick. For a second she was reluctant to sit down, convinced he would pull the chair out from under her the way Mike always did.

But Peter gently pressed on her shoulder with his palms, and she sat as he pushed the chair closer to the table.

"You see," Uncle Ben continued. "May can hear anything. It's uncanny. She can hear the neighbor's squabbles, chatter from airplanes overhead," he passed the bread to Mary Jane.

They continued a light banter as Mary Jane stared at her plate. She couldn't possibly eat this! All thoughts of Peter, of what had just happened in the basement, of the conversation around her vanished.

In her mind she tallied up the calories. The bread was about a hundred a slice, not including butter. Vegetables were probably okay, yet she wasn't sure. They were all tossed together, and she suspected some sort of oil dressing was used for flavor. Maybe she could scrape it off, or nibble on pieces without any dressing. Maybe.

But the casserole! There were potato chips layered on the top, probably mayonnaise or cheese or something equally gooey holding it all together.

But it smelled so good. She felt her stomach rumble, and hoped it wouldn't be loud enough for everyone to hear. Especially Aunt May with her sonar ears.

But tomorrow was class with Madame Olga.

*Ve do not vont ze tubby dancers, non?*

"And for dessert I've made apple cobbler with whipped cream," Aunt May plopped a massive serving of the casserole on her plate. "So eat up."

Mary Jane tried, she really tried. But the best she could manage was a few bites of the vegetables and moving the casserole from side to side on the plate.

Peter was watching her, and she thought she saw him exchange glances with Aunt May, but maybe she was just being paranoid. Her whole world, it seemed, was focused on the one stupid plate of food.

How could something so innocuous seem so menacing?

Uncle Ben was talking about seeing a concert with Benny Goodman when he was about their age. About the dances they did as kids, the Lindy Hop. Something about zoot suits and fedoras. Mary Jane listened, pushing the food around. She tried to concentrate on his features. Uncle Ben was wonderfully kind, his face worn by the sun. At his ears there were little swirls, like the markings waves make in the sand, as if measuring the decades.

Everyone else sat with an empty plate, Peter helping himself to seconds. She noticed that he managed to use the utensils without touching them to his fingertips. The conversation continued. Now the casserole was clotted, and the very sight sickened her.

She managed to avoid dessert by claiming to be too stuffed, and it wasn't a lie. Even the small amount of food she had consumed that night was more than she had eaten in days. And for the first time, she thought it might be a good idea to throw it up when she got home.

Part of her was aware this was crossing a dangerous line. But she was just feeling so full, so uncomfortable, so disgusted with herself, she didn't want to dwell on the negatives.

*Ve do not vont ze tubby dancers, non?*

"So Mary Jane," Uncle Ben announced. "Let me know when you want me to drive you home."

"Oh, thanks, Uncle Ben," said Peter. "But MJ and I have more work to do. I'll take her home myself later."

"No, Peter," she rushed. "Actually, I would like to get home now, as soon as possible."

"But Mary Jane, I thought..."

She stood up. "Thank you so much for dinner, it was wonderful!" She began to stack the dishes.

"Honey, no need to do that," Aunt May placed a hand on her arm. "We have an automatic dishwasher right here," she gestured to Peter.

"Well," Uncle Ben stood. "Why don't I drive Mary Jane home while Peter finishes up the dishes?"

"Uncle Ben, I..." Peter began.

"Oh, thank you! That would be great!"

Peter stared at her, then shook his head. "Sure. No problem. I'll run downstairs and get your book bag."

She couldn't wait to get home. All she could think about was getting rid of all that extra fat, all the calories. And every stoplight and delay would make the ugly fat stick to her, make it stay forever. Bulge from her leotards, ripple from her tights.

Then, about a block from her home, as Uncle Ben chatted pleasantly, she realized she'd left her ballet stuff back at the Parkers'.

No matter. She had an extra set for tomorrow, and she didn't want to waste the precious time traveling all the way back, letting the fat get a toehold. Then it would never go away. She just knew it.

"Thank you so much, Mr. Parker," she said as he pulled up to her house.

"Just call me Uncle Ben," he got out and opened the car door for her. "Good night."

"'Night!" she called as she ran into the house.

She fumbled with the keys, hands trembling. No one was at home. Mary Jane threw down her book bag in the hallway, and headed straight for the bathroom.

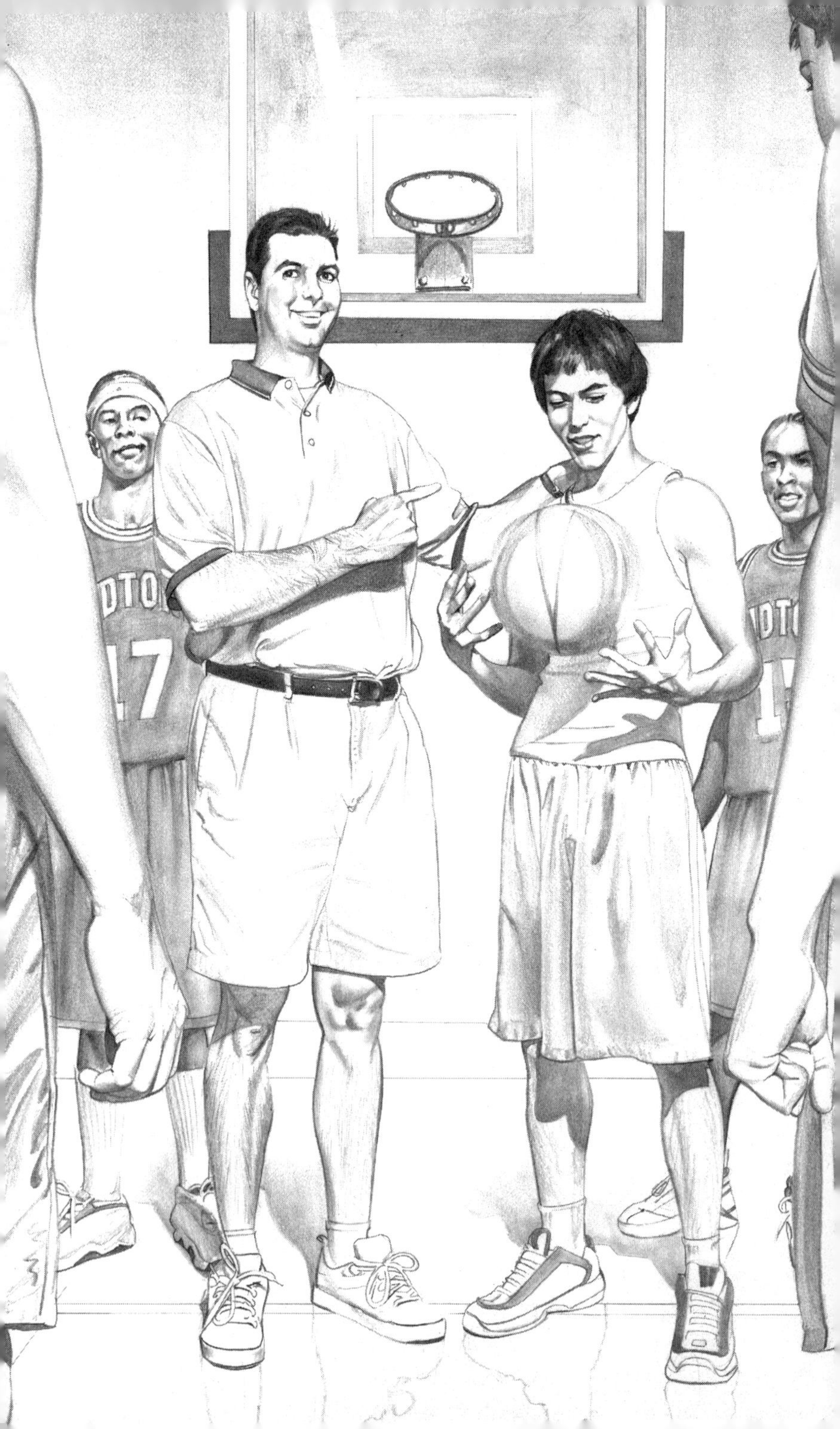

# chapter 4

Wendy and Alison were right. Coach Renny was actively recruiting Peter Parker for basketball. It wasn't a particularly hard sell. Peter was apparently delighted to be recruited by the coach. He started in his first game after only one practice. Within a few days, he became the athletic department's new pet, leaving a befuddled Flash with a stunned, deer-in-headlights expression.

"Parker is just a jerk," he muttered to no one in particular. "He's a real jerk," he said in a slightly louder voice.

But no one was listening, simply because the entire campus was busy recruiting Peter Parker for one thing or another.

Suddenly, he was everywhere. The other jocks oohed and ahhed over his Herculean prowess.

"Man, did you see that? The dude just bench pressed two fifty without even a groan!"

"I was spotting for him," preened the first string quarterback.

"He's such a jerk," added Flash.

The cool, non-athletic kids—the smart ones who

edited the school newspaper or played in the hipper garage bands—embraced him as one of their own.

"Yeah, I'm having a party Saturday night. We're doing a poetry slam, and Peter Parker might come." There was no actual evidence that he would attend. But there was an electric charge of hope that it was possible.

The computer geeks played "remember when," as in, "Remember last year, when Peter Parker was the recording secretary of the electronics club, and he used to eat lunch with us sometimes?"

Even the faculty seemed dazzled by his dramatic metamorphosis. "I have sent Mr. Parker some pamphlets on my college alma mater," sniffed Mr. Ashworth, the principal, while sipping bad coffee in the teacher's lounge.

"So did I," admitted Miss Ingram.

Coach Renny didn't mention that he, too, had forwarded some information on his community college, as had the drivers' education instructor, the volley ball coach, and the home economics teacher who, while she never actually had Peter as a student, wanted her old college to think she did. For this was a kid who was going places. This was a kid who would certainly make a name for himself and, by some sort of osmosis, anyone associated with his budding greatness.

"All he's done so far is make a few baskets in a couple of games and get rid of his glasses," Mary Jane shrugged to Wendy. "What's the big deal?"

"The big deal? Other than the fact that he's drop

dead gorgeous and has become the new wonderboy of the b-ball team? Other than the simple fact that he made forty some-odd points in the last game?"

"Frankly, yeah. He's still the same person he always was. He's just no longer optically challenged. That's probably the whole change. No glasses, and Clark Kent becomes Superman. Everyone else was just a dumb Lois for not seeing the real Clark."

"Give me a break, MJ. Face reality. Appearances are everything, or just about everything. And...wait! Look who's coming over here!"

"Who?" Mary Jane was still thinking about what Wendy just said. That appearances were everything.

And the terrible thing was that Wendy was right.

Everyone wanted a piece of Peter Parker. Why? Because he was smart, maybe. That was only a small part of it. He had always been smart. The only difference was that now he had become the school hottie.

The difference between popularity and dorkdom was a couple of well-developed muscles and even facial features. Looks are everything. Appearances define all else. Brains are fine, as long as they are packaged so they don't show.

Wendy was chattering about something. And all Mary Jane could hear was a droning buzz, a loud, meaningless white sound.

So now Peter was the accessory of choice. Now everyone wanted him.

And no group was more aggressive in their pursuit of Peter Parker than the female population of Midtown High. Mary Jane had thought the quest for Harry Osborn had been intense. Compared to the way girls threw themselves at Peter, the Harry Osborn chase had been amateur hour.

She looked up, and there he was, Peter Parker. Man of the Hour. He was strolling down the hall like a politician or a game show host, making casual conversation with what seemed to be the entire cheerleading squad.

His immediate circle was first tier, the varsity football and basketball cheerleaders. There was a weird flip in her stomach, as if she had just dropped two floors in an elevator.

Peter was surrounded by gorgeous girls. They were a flash of blond, shiny hair and whiter-than-white teeth, all encased in too-tight sweaters and too-tall heels. Just beyond the teenage goddesses were the soccer cheerleaders and pom pom girls. Some had brownish hair, but most were sunkissed, or peroxide kissed, and they were tantalizingly close to being mistaken for football cheerleaders at thirty paces. Trailing behind were the wrestling cheerleaders, or Mat Maids, a more normal-looking group of girls. One even had freckles, while another took a bold fashion U-turn with a faded "Grateful Dead" tee-shirt.

At least they don't look like some Aryan genetic experiment gone mad.

"Hey there, gorgeous." For a moment Mary Jane thought it was Peter. Hoped it was Peter. But it wasn't. He was still bobbing in the sea-o-babes.

"Oh, hi Flash. How's it going?"

"Great. Listen, a bunch of us are getting together to go to Wrestle Cage Rage this weekend. Wanna come along?"

"I don't know. I'm not really much of a wrestling fan." She couldn't help but notice one of the cheerleaders licked Peter's face, actually licked it!

"Oh, yeah. I'm not either. It's really stupid. But on Saturday the Demon Knife Master takes on anyone who dares to wrestle him."

"Why would anyone do that?" Mary Jane watched Peter as he accepted a sip from a bottle of OZ offered by Brittany Boobs. Boobs was not her real last name. Brittany probably wasn't her real name either. But it was what Wendy and MJ had christened her, the fake name to go with the fake...

"...and Parker's going. The jerk. Anyway, they give a thousand bucks a minute to anyone who can survive the Demon Knife Master. So far no one's gone beyond thirty seconds. This one guy flipped over and landed in the audience! It was awesome! Another time DKM took this skinny headbanger and really banged his head. Once..."

"Peter's going? Well, maybe it might be sort of fun."

Flash clenched a fist. "Yeah. Parker's going to grace us with his almighty presence."

"God, Watson, where've you been?" Wendy gave her a duh shake of her head. "I just told you about Saturday night. Didn't you hear me?"

"Oh, sure."

"She's just all hot and heavy to be with Parker," Flash growled.

"I am not!" Mary Jane began to protest.

And suddenly Peter was there.

"Hey, guys," he said looking around at all the faces, as if greeting everyone by their name would take too much time.

"Hi. Listen, Peter, we really have to get together to work on that project." Mary Jane couldn't help but notice that the bottle Brittany had offered was stamped with red crescent lipstick smears. When Peter took his swallow, he, too, had a splotch of lipstick on his upper lip.

"Yeah, sure, MJ," he grinned.

She smiled, too, not wanting to mention that he was now wearing a coat of Passion Rose.

"Hey," he continued, his smile broadening. "A bunch of us are going to Wrestle Rage Cage on..."

"It's Wrestle Cage Rage, dude," snapped Flash. "And I already asked her."

"Why, Flash. How clever of you to know your Rages from your Cages," Peter raised his eyebrows as if genuinely impressed.

"Jerk," Flash hissed as he began to leave.

"What did you say?" Peter's tone was no longer light.

"Nothing," Flash said the words as if it was a vile curse.

"What's your problem?" Peter egged him on.

"Come on, guys," Mary Jane was eager to separate them. "Hey, Peter. How about this afternoon for the project? I have some ideas and..."

Flash again said something. At first she thought Peter hadn't heard. Then he spoke with a low, menacing voice. "What did you say, Flash? Cage or Rage?"

By now there was a small crowd circled around the two boys. Flash was visibly nervous, but Mary Jane could see he couldn't possibly back down without losing face.

Flash's eyes darted around the crowd, surveying the faces, hoping for a friendly one.

But at that moment he was all alone.

"I just said," he repeated loudly. "I said that you look lovely in that lipstick."

Peter stared at him. Mary Jane, Wendy, the varying degrees of cheerleaders and the other bystanders held their collective breath.

Then Peter did the utterly unexpected. He wiped the back of his hand against his mouth, then looked at it. "Nice. Is that a Skye Bleu shade, Mary Jane?"

"Yes. Passion Rose, I believe." Everyone breathed a silent sigh of relief, although a few of the disappointed frowned at the lack of bloodshed. The excitement was over. One or two of the fringe of on-lookers began heading to their next class.

When suddenly, Flash leapt at Peter.

Instead of fighting back, Peter jumped back from the first few swings. Then, with his palm he pressed Flash by the forehead, the other teen thrashing wildly in the air. But Flash continued to propel himself forward, as if ramming a football dummy in practice. A few people laughed uncomfortably.

"This is ridiculous," Peter shook his head.

"I am not ridiculous!" Spittle flew from his mouth.

Flash hauled his fist back, almost in slow motion, as if to deliver one mighty blow.

And he nailed Mary Jane on the cheek.

"Oh!" She staggered back, hand over her face, and knocked loudly into the lockers. Her eyes were already beginning to tear.

"MJ!" The slamming pop of Flash's clenched fist connecting with Peter's open hand was deafening.

"Ouch!" Flash cried, crumpling into a low crouch as he cradled his right hand. "Man, I think it's broken! He broke my hand!"

Nobody came to his side. Nobody came to Mary Jane or Peter. Instead they just stared, wide-eyed, the whole group with the same expression of stunned surprise.

"Mary Jane, are you okay?" Peter rushed to her side.

An adult voice pierced the chaos. "What's going on here?" It was Vice Principal Van Arsdale pushing his way through the spectators.

"Parker broke my hand!" Flash cried.

Van Arsdale grabbed Peter by the collar, then did the same to Flash, with an expression of annoyance similar to that of an animal control agent invading a nest of pesky vermin. "Both of you jokers are coming with me."

Peter pushed him away. "Wait a minute. Please...Mary Jane, are you okay?"

Numbly she nodded, ignoring the hot, stinging pain on her face.

The vice principal tightened his grip and dragged the two boys to his office, as Wendy took Mary Jane to the nurse for some ice.

The bell rang, and silently, with wary glances at each other and perplexed shakes of their heads, everyone went to class.

\* \* \*

*Dear Diary,*

*It's been a long time since I've written in this thing. Good: I've dropped over fifteen pounds and think I'm ready to try out for the varsity cheerleading squad. Missy Lewis is moving to California, so there's a space. Should I dye my hair blond to improve the chances? Maybe!*

*Bad: Mom is still hanging with Mike the Moron. I hate him. Total creep. Also bad: Seems as if my dancing days are over. Mom can't afford it anymore. Maybe if she stopped springing for Mike and his beer, her Skye Bleu salary would go further.*

*Haven't seen much of Peter lately. He's been busy. Saw a movie with Harry Osborn the other night. Afterwards we drove by his place. Wow. The place is a palace! I thought poor Harry was going to sink into the seat when his dad came out to meet us in a silk smoking jacket, like something straight out of one of those British plays on PBS. I was waiting for him to ring for Jeeves.*

*Guess the old guy has issues. After all, his first name is Norman. You'd think someone with all that money and power could afford a better first name.*

*I'm heading over to Peter's tonight to work on the project, provided, of course, that he's not still incarcerated in the vice principal's office.*

\* \* \*

Aunt May hugged Mary Jane when she entered the hallway. "My dear, how have you been?"

"Fine. Thank you." She backed away, uncomfortable at being touched so closely.

"Why, Mary Jane! You're nothing but skin and bones."

"I guess I'm going through some sort of growth spurt."

"You and Peter. I swear, that boy seems to have grown a foot in the past couple of weeks. He's downstairs in the lab. Would you like anything to eat or drink?"

"No thank you. I'll just go downstairs."

Part of her felt guilty at leaving Aunt May so quickly. She was such a nice lady, and she really didn't mean any harm. It's just that Mary Jane was feeling some strong anti-adult feelings lately. Everyone, from her mother on, seemed to let her down. The more she hoped for, the less she got.

The cellar door was partially open as she headed down the steps.

Why couldn't she work at Ruby's so she could continue her dance lessons? She had offered to do anything, from helping with the kids' class, to answering the phones—even sweeping the studio floor. But Ruby had said they really didn't need the help. What they needed were more paying students.

Then she paused at the foot of the steps. The lab seemed to be empty, yet she had the eerie sensation of not being alone. The hair on her arms prickled.

Something was very wrong.

"Peter?"

From someplace above was a scrambling sound, like a large animal scurrying. And she saw the briefest of flickering movement from the ceiling.

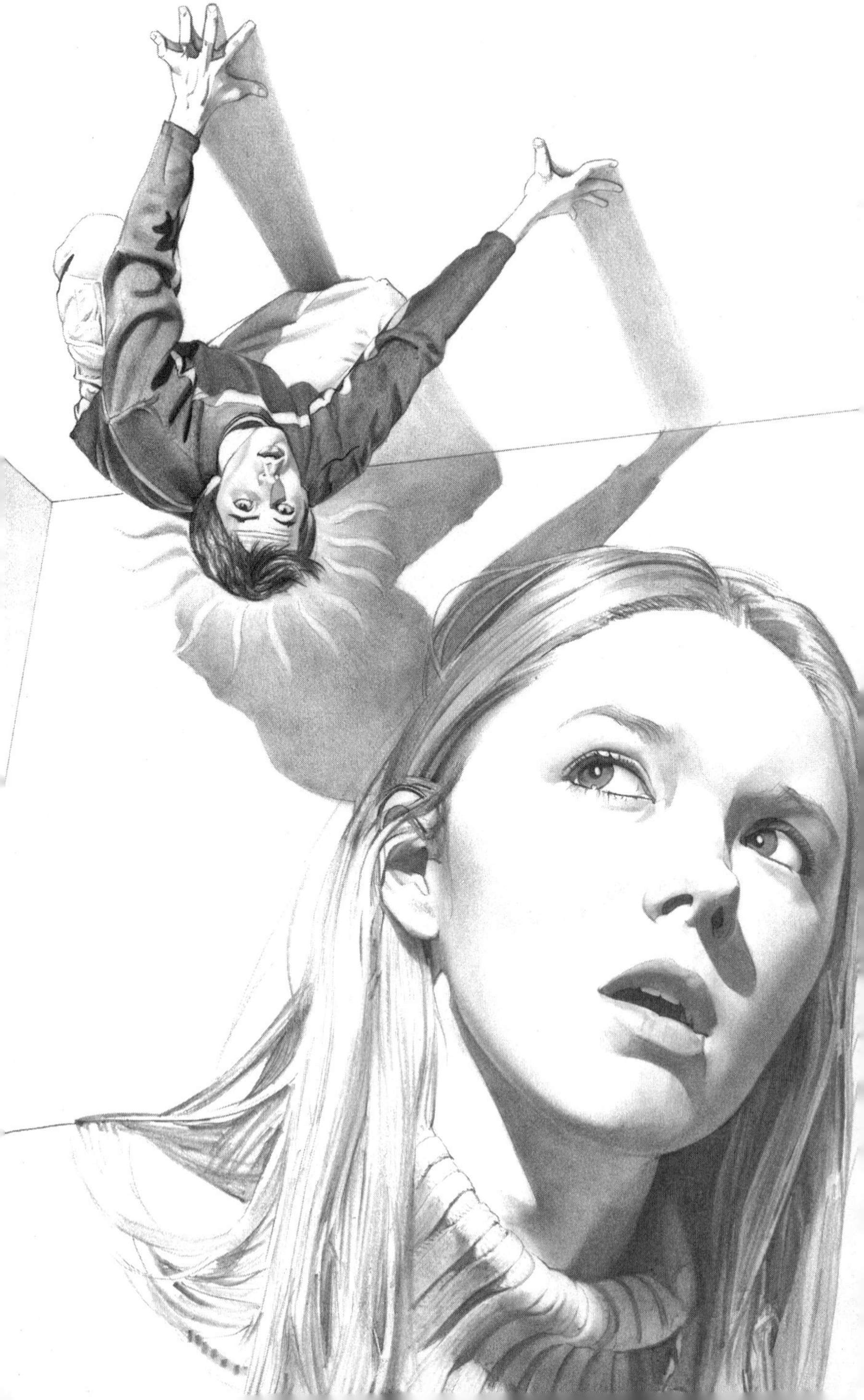

"Peter, where are you?" Her voice took on that high-pitched tone she so disliked.

"Um, I'm over here." Then he emerged from behind a bookshelf, his face slightly red.

"Were you just on the ceiling?"

"God, MJ, what the hell would I be doing on the ceiling?"

"I don't know." She put down her book bag. "Stranger things have been happening, if you know what I mean."

For a moment he did not say anything. Then he took a deep breath. "Yeah. I know. Hey, how's your cheek?"

"It hurts, but the nurse said it's just bruised. What happened with you guys after the brawl?"

"I wouldn't call it a brawl."

"What would you call it then? Wendy said she saw Flash later with a cast on his hand. If it's not a brawl, it's just a conversation in which someone happened to break a hand?"

"Okay, whatever. Flash and I are both suspended for three days."

"You're kidding!"

"Nope."

"Wow. Peter Parker, suspended. Very impressive. Hey, what about Friday's basketball game against Brooklyn Tech? Can you still play?"

"Funny about that. Van Arsdale made it clear that I am suspended from classes, but am expected at practice and the games. Great guy, that Van Arsdale. He has his priorities straight."

She smiled. "Sure sounds like it."

Then Peter looked at his watch. "Don't you have ballet?"

"Nah. Mom can't pay for the lessons anymore. Not that it's such a great dance school or anything."

"I'm sorry, MJ. That sucks. That will leave you with lots of spare time, at least. Unless..." He crossed his arms.

"Unless what?"

"Why don't you try out for the cheerleading squad? Missy Lewis is moving away. It might be fun."

"Well, I don't know. Maybe."

"I'll bet you could handle the moves with all that ballet experience of yours."

She was afraid to admit she had been thinking just the same thing.

"Hey, I've got an idea!" Peter brightened. "Why don't you show me a few moves? I mean, I've seen enough of the cheerleaders to know what they have to do. I'll show you how to be the next Missy Lewis."

"Yeah. Everyone knows you've seen a lot of the cheerleaders," she grinned. "Anyway, let's get to work on this science project."

"Show me a move."

"Come on, Peter. Really. This is stupid."

"Show me."

"There's not enough room. Really, let's just..."

With that he pushed aside a huge, old-fashioned heavy desk and two folding chairs.

Now she was ticked. "Fine. Move out of the way."

He crossed his arms, an amused grin on his face.

"I'm serious, Peter," she raised her arms, ready to do a cartwheel. "I'll take you out."

He refused to move.

So with one skip, she launched into a cartwheel, a flip, and only by a fast side-step did Peter avoid being trampled by her final leaping mid-air split.

"Wow! How did you do that without crashing into the bookshelves?"

"Simple. Once you know exactly how much room you need, you can make small adjustments and avoid the ugly crash."

"Impressive. You look like a road show of *Charlie's Angels*. Hey, can you show me how to do that?"

"Why?" She was unable to keep from laughing.

"Because, well. Because it might help me in basketball. Coach says I'm a little wild."

"You sure he's talking about your on-court action?"

"Very funny. But really, can you show me just a few of those?"

She agreed, and Peter proved to be a surprisingly fast learner, although he refused to really practice in front of her. He watched her intently, mirroring her movements but not following through with complete springs or jumps.

"I'll work on those later," he was barely breaking a sweat, while she was panting. "Oh, here. You must be thirsty. Want an OZ? I nabbed a few for the project, and Coach gave me a bunch to drink."

"Don't you want to figure out what's in it first?"

"Well, I figure it has to be safe. I mean, Harry's been drinking it for weeks. It's pretty good stuff. I like the citrus flavor, but the berry flavor leaves your tongue blue for days. You end up looking like a strangled chow. You might have to get used to it if you join the cheerleaders."

Mary Jane looked at the bottle, a kid-friendly label with a multi-colored rainbow plastered on the side. But then something caught her eye—two hundred and eighty calories per serving! Servings per container: 2.6!

"Ugh, no thanks," she handed it back.

"You didn't even try it?"

"Really, no thanks. Let's just get to work and figure out what the hell is in it."

"Aren't you hungry?"

"Nah. I ate already. Here, let me get my folder."

He studied her a moment. "Mary Jane?"

"Yeah?" She looked up at him, a half smile on her face.

He paused, then he, too, smiled. "Nothing."

Then they got to some serious work. First they went through all of the ingredients on the label, testing for each one and checking off the properties. But they found some odd amino acid combinations they couldn't identify through the preliminary diagnostics they had conducted. Hopes for an easy "A" retreated as they started devising a new battery of tests. It was going to be a long night.

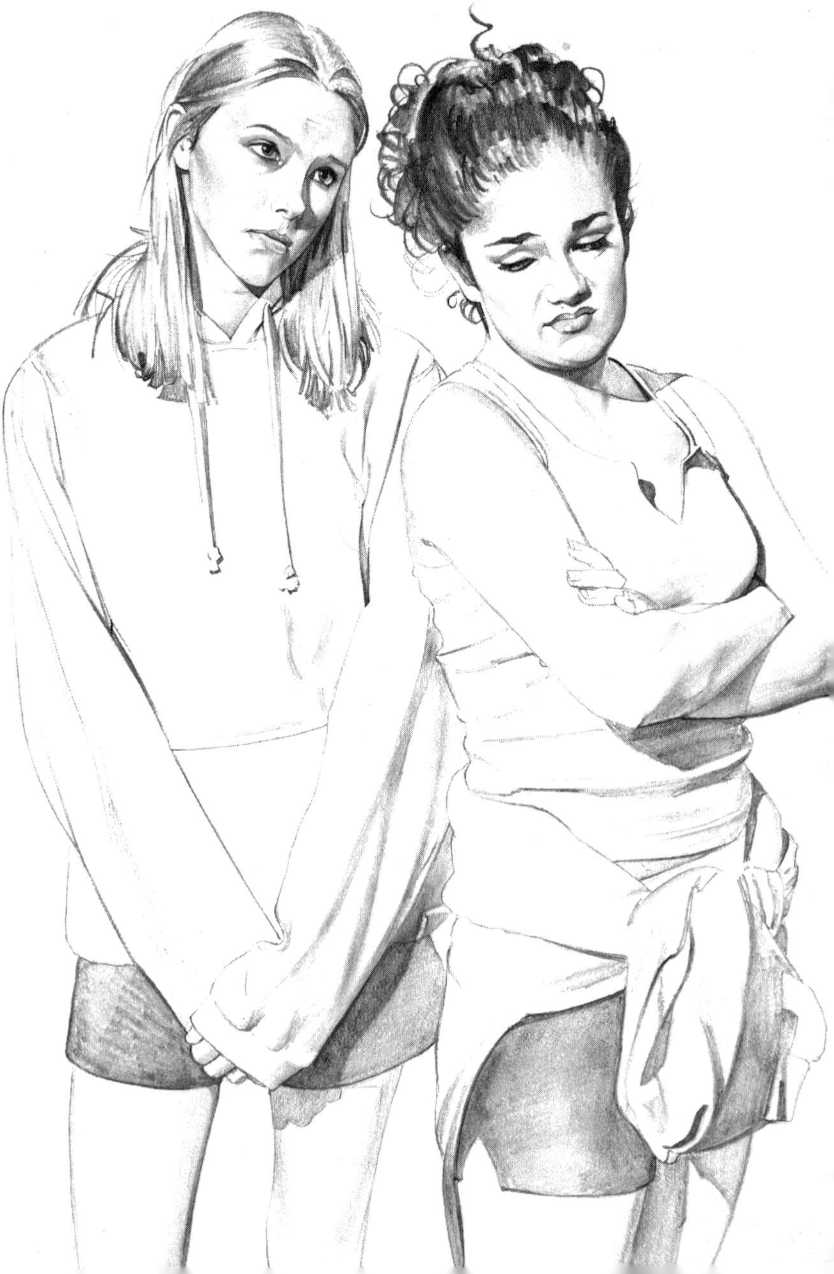

# chapter 5

Madeline Watson tapped her foot and waited for her daughter to walk through the door.

She glanced up at the plastic wall clock in the kitchen. It was just after eleven, on a school night. And Madeline had no idea where Mary Jane was, or when—even if—she was returning home that evening.

She reached for the telephone, about to call Wendy's house. Then she hesitated. Maybe Mary Jane had indeed told her where she would be, but she had forgotten. Work had been so difficult, so time consuming, that she realized somewhere along the line she had put being a mother on hold.

A haunting thought came to her then.

When had she not put being a mother on hold? Left her daughter in the care of others, or more recently to fend for herself?

"What she needs is a good smack," growled Mike from his perch on the couch. From the kitchen she could hear the distinctive pop of another beer can, followed by his trademark slurp. "That's exactly what she needs. A smack."

Madeline looked at him pleadingly. "Please, Mike. She's my daughter. Let me handle her. Maybe it would be best if you just left now."

"You just can't handle her. Just like you had to hire me to track down that deadbeat ex of yours, you have no spine, no..."

"Get out." Madeline said softly. "Please, go now."

"What?"

"I need to speak to my daughter alone. Please leave."

"Come on, now. You're just..."

Then the front door opened, and Mary Jane entered, her mouth a small "o" of surprise when she saw her mother standing in the kitchen. Mike was there.

Before she could speak, her mother folded her arms. "Go now, Mike."

Mary Jane's eyes widened.

Mike, looking very much as if he wanted to say something, grabbed his jacket and left.

"Mom! I can't believe you just tossed Mike out!"

Madeline took a deep breath. "I can't either..." Then she straightened. "Where have you been? I've been worried out of my mind about you!" Concern made her voice sharper than she had intended. "Don't even bother telling me you were at your ballet class."

"I won't. How could I? They don't give away lessons, not even at Ruby's House-O-Dance."

Her mother flushed red, and immediately Mary Jane regretted her words. "Mom, listen. I'm sorry. I..."

"Where were you?"

"I was over at Peter's working on our science project."

"Oh." Madeline closed her eyes. In that unguarded moment, Mary Jane was startled by how very vulnerable her mother looked. Not just slender, no—beyond that—skinny. She looked so lost, so very unhappy. Before she could scrutinize her mother further, she opened her eyes. Once again she was the inquiring parent. "How is the project going?"

"Pretty well." Swinging her backpack over her shoulder, Mary Jane began to head to her bedroom. "Oh, Mom. I might be late tomorrow as well. Cheerleading tryouts."

"Really?" Her mother brightened. "That's wonderful! You know, most Miss Americas were on their high school cheerleading squads. That's a fact."

"Is it?" Mary Jane replied, uncertain of how to react to such unstartling news.

"Yes, it is. I'm fairly certain, in any case. There were probably a few exceptions, like that deaf girl a couple of years back. I don't think she was a cheerleader."

Exhausted, Mary Jane simply smiled. "Great. Thanks. Well, good night." She paused. "Mom, are you okay?"

"Yes, I think I am. Good night, dear," Madeline returned the smile. "And in case I don't see you tomorrow morning, good luck with the tryouts."

With much relief, Mary Jane escaped to her small bedroom, closing the door behind her and wishing she could block out the rest of the world just as easily.

\* \* \*

By the time of the afternoon tryouts, Mary Jane was feeling strong, confident. All she'd eaten since the day before was a piece of dry toast and a small can of tomato juice. Only a hundred and thirty calories, max.

Wouldn't Madame Olga be proud?

*Ve do not vont zee tubby cheerleaders.*

There were at least a dozen other girls clustered around the gymnasium door, all awaiting the signal from Miss Downey, the cheerleading coach and occasional global studies teacher. Mary Jane felt good. After a quick scan of the rear ends of the girls in front of her, she knew she by far was the skinniest one there.

It was difficult to keep a satisfied grin from her face.

"MJ?" A familiar voice. "Mary Jane?"

"Wendy! What are you doing here?"

"Trying out for the squad."

"You're kidding?"

"No, I'm not. Why? You don't think I have a chance?"

"That's not what I mean," she exclaimed.

"You're not exactly blond yourself, chiquita."

A sudden, irrational fury rose in Mary Jane.

"Yeah, but at least I've studied dance for years," she snapped. "I know what I'm doing. I know how to move." There was intensity to her voice that was as vicious as it was unintended.

The smile fell from Wendy's face, the fun left her eyes. "Back off." For a moment, just a moment, her chin trembled, then she straightened her shoulders. "God, when did you turn into such a bitch?"

Stunned, Mary Jane shook her head. "Oh, Wendy! I'm so sorry. I don't know where that came from. Really..."

Wendy stared for a few moments, then she turned and walked away, joining a cluster of other girls.

She's just jealous. That's it. She knows I'll get the one spot on the cheerleading squad.

But she is also a friend, someone who has been there for me. A real friend.

"Wendy!" she called, just as the double doors to the gym opened. The tryouts were about to begin. Mary Jane took a deep breath and focused.

Three hours later, Miss Downey announced the newest member of the varsity cheerleading team: Mary Jane Watson.

And strangely, all Mary Jane could feel was a gnawing emptiness.

\* \* \*

Harry Osborn was the first to ask the newly minted cheerleader out on an official date.

"Congrats, MJ," he used his most sensual, I-can-pick-up-any-chick-anytime-anywhere tone. "How would you like to catch a flick this weekend?"

"Sure, Harry," she said trying to catch up with Wendy, who was already down the street. She desperately needed to speak to her, to say how sorry she was about how she had behaved.

When did you turn into such a bitch?

"You going to the wrestling thing tonight with the gang?"

"Um, yeah. Sure."

"Great. I'll see you there."

"Fine." Wendy had already turned the corner.

She'll be there tonight, at wrestling. Maybe I can apologize then.

Harry said something else before he left, although she didn't pay any attention. A few other guys stopped her as she walked alone, one asking what she thought of the calculus homework (was he even in her class?), another if she had heard the new Eminem CD (like she cared).

"Mary Jane." Peter seemed to step from nowhere.

"Peter," she beamed, waiting for him to congratulate her on making the squad. He of all people knew what a very big deal this was. "I thought you were suspended?"

"I'm here for basketball practice. How are you doing?" Odd. He wasn't smiling.

"Great!"

"Oh. I'm glad to hear that. I've been worried about you."

"What are you talking about?"

"Listen, MJ, and really listen. I know you're having a tough time. I wanted to talk about it last night, but between our acrobatics and the project, I didn't...anyway, the point is, I think you're in trouble."

"You're crazy. I'm not the one who got suspended for fighting," she spun to leave, and he grabbed her arm. For a moment, perhaps because of the sudden movement, she was dizzy, and he steadied her with astonishing strength. She stared down at the grip he had on her. His one hand felt like a vise.

"You are not eating, Mary Jane. I know that because I've been with you, seen you push around your food."

"Maybe I just don't like your aunt's cooking." Her voice was harsh, cruel, and she was unable to meet his eyes.

But he didn't react. "When I saw you from across the yard, I couldn't believe who it was. You must have dropped close to fifteen pounds."

Eighteen, but who's counting?

"And you didn't need to lose weight anyway. Please listen to me, Mary Jane."

"You're just mad because now I'm popular."

"No. I'm just mad because you look like crap, your hair is falling out, and your breath stinks because you never eat."

"You're lying!"

"Do you know what some of the guys are calling you?"

"That's why you're mad! Because some of the guys are calling me!"

Her eyes were bright, and he relaxed his grip on her. "Listen to me. A bunch of the guys have a nickname for you. Do you know what it is?"

It was hard for her to speak, his face so close to hers. Self-conscious—did she really have bad breath? She shook her head.

For the first time he hesitated. He turned his head away briefly, then looked back at her. "They call you 'Rex.'"

Again she felt dizzy, as if she was bobbing on a wave. "Rex? Why that? I don't get it."

Then, very gently, he let her go, careful she didn't stumble. "Oh, Mary Jane. They call you that because it's short for 'Anorexia.' Rex. Get it?"

"Well," she began slowly. "That's a compliment, really. I mean, it's better to be too slender than too fat, right?"

"You left the land of slender ten pounds ago. Now you're just skinny."

A strange sense of elation ran through her. He noticed! They all noticed her hard work!

"That's why I made the cheerleading squad," she said with triumph. "They needed someone light to be on top of the pyramid, and I was the lightest! Did you know I made the squad?"

"Yeah, I know." He started to walk away, shaking his head. "Wendy told me."

"Really? Did she say anything else? She tried out but didn't make it."

"I've gotta go, MJ. We'll work on the project in a few days, okay?"

Then he just walked away.

* * *

Peter was, of course, the star of Friday's basketball game against arch rivals Brooklyn Tech. Both Mary Jane and Flash were forced to sit on the sidelines, MJ because Missy Lewis was still there and she had yet to learn all of the routines. Flash was on the bench because Peter Parker was the new athletic sensation and the fans on both sides demanded to see him perform.

That, and the minor fact that Flash's right hand was broken in three places and encased in a thick plaster cast.

"The jerk," he said to himself when Peter made a spectacular basket from the other side of the court.

"That's his forty-eighth point this game, right?"

Even the Tech fans were cheering for him.

Mary Jane looked across the court at the spectators, watching their reaction to Peter. And then she saw someone....could it be?

What was Norman Osborn doing at the basketball game?

She looked harder. He seemed to be talking with someone who looked like the head clipboard person at Osborn Industries.

"Hey, gorgeous," Harry Osborn slid on the bench behind them and tugged on Mary Jane's hair.

"Hi, Harry," Flash replied. "Parker's really making a jerk out of himself out there."

"Man, did you see that?" Harry shouted. "How'd he do that? I've never seen anyone jump that high without special effects!"

"Harry, is that your father over there?"

Harry looked in the direction she was pointing. "I don't see him. Where?"

"I could have sworn I just saw him, just under the big sign that says..."

But he wasn't there.

"Nah, I doubt he'd be here anyway," Harry said. "Dad's got some big meeting or something over at his office."

There was another wild roar as Peter scored another basket. "Fifty points right?" She shouted. "Yeah, Peter's really humiliating himself."

Someone tapped Mary Jane on the shoulder. It was a cheerleader, although Mary Jane wasn't quite sure of her name.

"Mary Jane? Hi. One of the other cheerleaders just

hurt her ankle and can't do the pyramid. Can you change in the locker room and join us at half-time?"

"But I don't know the whole routine yet!"

"You know enough. Hey, you were great the other day at the try-out. You caught on really fast. Come on, we really need you."

"Go on, MJ," Harry urged. Flash said nothing other than a muttered "Fifty-four" at Peter's last basket—and at his plaster cast.

It all happened so quickly! One moment she was on the bench, the next she was running through the crowds to get to the girls' locker room. Miss Downey was there.

"Oh, Mary Jane! Thank goodness!" Her tongue was blue, as were the tongues of half the smiling girls on the squad.

"Miss Downey, I'm not sure I can do this!" But they were already pulling her sweater over her head and someone had a little cheerleader sweater and pleated skirt.

"You'll be an anchor this time, the base of the pyramid," Miss Downey was explaining. "Just follow the other girls, especially LaShonda. She's your mirror opposite. Do whatever she does, only not. Got it?"

"Yeah. It's a snap. Ouch!"

"Sorry! Your earring caught on the collar," LaShonda rushed. "We have to hurry!"

"Shoes!" Miss Downey yelled. "Wait, there's no time. You'll just have to wear what you have on!

Now out there and have fun! Everyone," she clapped. "Go do it!"

And suddenly she was out in the middle of the basketball court, clapping her hands and mouthing a spirited cheer. From the corner of her eye she watched LaShonda, matching her move for move.

The crowds were cheering with approval, stomping their feet as one. It was a mad, awesome thrill of pure euphoria! She saw faces as blurs, mouths opened wide in exaggerated shouts. Paper banners stretched across the gym, brightly painted with brilliant rainbows and "Go Team!" Hands were raised, also blurs, flashes of color. Everyone's eyes were shining, glassy with joy.

"Ready, set!" One of the girls called the cue to start the formation. And Mary Jane moved in unison with the others, the rapid shuffle of feet as everyone got into position. LaShonda bent to the side, and Mary Jane did the same, placing her thigh in an extended pose like a step. Then Missy Lewis began her rapid climb. She scrambled to the top.

A weird sensation wafted over Mary Jane as she tried to hold her place. It was that bobbing-in-waves feeling.

I must keep my place. I can't let them down.

But her knees began to tremble, as if she'd been holding an arabesque for hours under hot lights.

Stay in position. Do not get sick.

That was the last thing she remembered.

* * *

"Mary Jane? MJ." Someone touched her hair.

Opening her eyes, she saw bright fluorescent lights, halos of pinkish haze encircling the bulb.

And then she saw Peter.

"What happened?" She began to sit up, and realized she was lying on one of the benches in the girls' locker room. "What are you doing in here?"

LaShonda leaned over her. "Are you okay? You just sort of keeled over, but don't worry. No one was hurt. And then, out of nowhere, Peter Parker swooped down and picked you up. Coach Renny was shouting at him, but he brought you in here anyway."

Peter helped her sit up.

"Don't you have to get back to the game?" She could hear the crowds cheer as if from a great distance.

"No way!" LaShonda exclaimed. "We're up by sixty points. So now Coach is playing everyone on the bench. Even the freshmen and that kid with the head gear. Oh, and Miss Downey says not to worry. You didn't drop anyone, and next time you'll be on the top anyway. Bye!"

Peter stood up. "Well, I've got to go."

"Thanks, Peter. Really, thank you. I'll catch ya later."

"Please, Mary Jane. Please think about why you fainted."

"I didn't faint. I just fell. Fell. It can happen to anybody."

"Right. Especially anybody who is starving themselves to death."

"Leave me alone. Please." For some reason she was close to tears. "Please."

"Okay. I'll see you then, at the wrestling thing."

All she could do is nod.

After he left she got dressed in her regular clothes, gave the cheerleading outfit back to Miss Downey, and let Harry Osborn take her home in the back of his limo.

And when he wanted to kiss her, she let him.

At least he didn't think she had stinky breath.

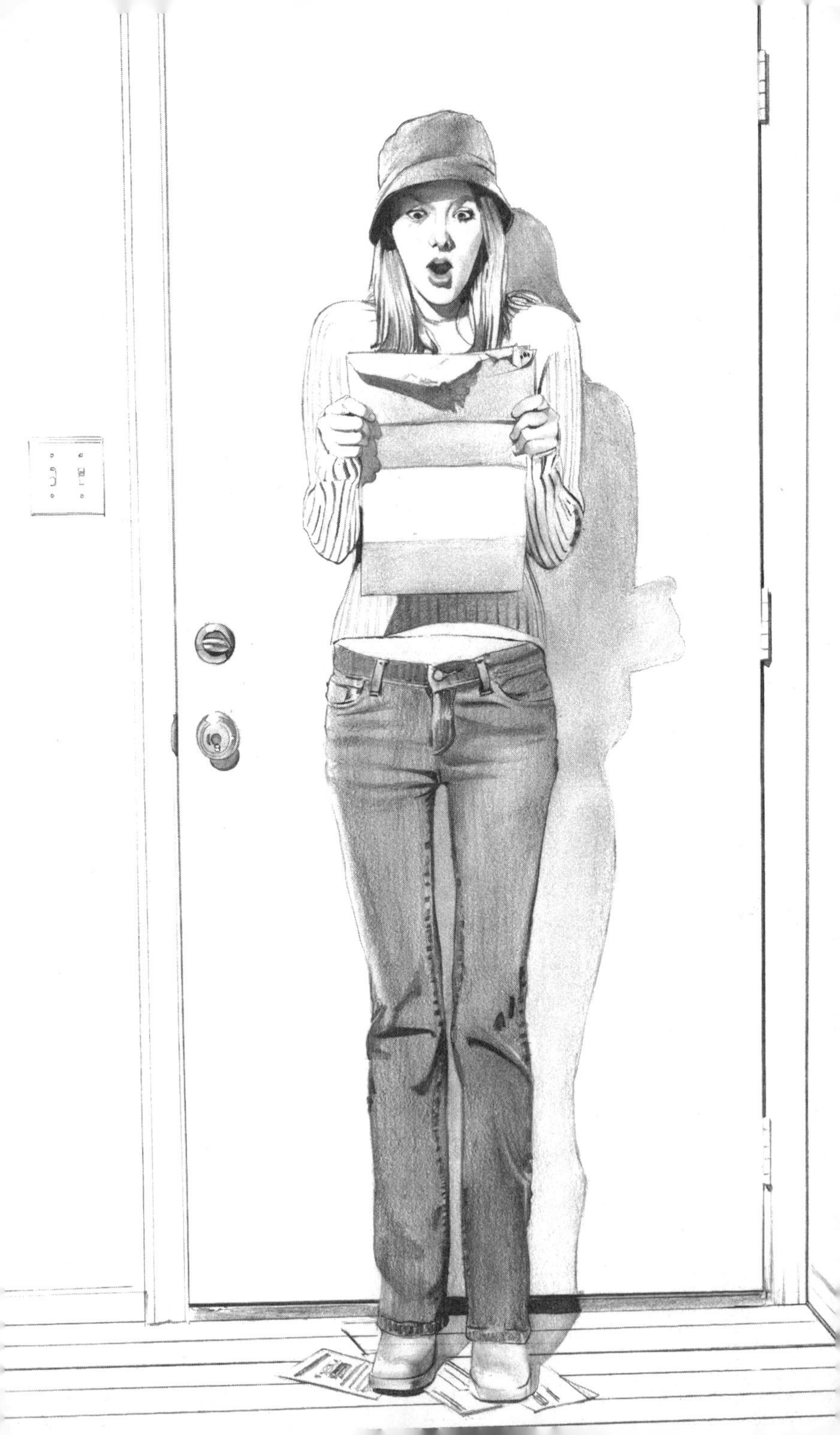

# chapter 6

There were worse things in the world, Mary Jane concluded, than having a date with an amazingly handsome, filthy-rich kid.

Harry grinned as the deafening sounds of Wrestle Cage Rage made conversation all but impossible.

And one of those worse things, she also concluded, was Wrestle Cage Rage.

It seemed almost impossible that thousands of men, women and children found a common interest in some creepy guy named the Demon Knife Master, or DKM to true aficionados. They demonstrated their devotion by wearing DKM tee-shirts (all several sizes too small), waving DKM foam rubber hands made to resemble circular saws, eating ice cream novelties with DKM's face stamped in milk chocolate, and—above all—by screaming.

Harry nudged her. "Isn't this great!" He shouted a mere two inches from her ear, yet she was forced to lip-read.

All she could do was nod.

On top of that, there were huge posters everywhere.

"Coming soon...OZ!" and "Brought to you by the makers of...OZ!"

This stuff was everywhere, and it wasn't even for sale yet!

Peter was a few seats away, and although he smiled and clapped and even took part in a Demon Knife Master stadium wave, his expression was slightly pained. She recognized that look, and was fairly certain she wore the same grimace.

He glanced at her, his smile wavering before he winked and offered a half-hearted thumbs up. In response she leaned closer to Harry, snuggling against his arm.

Peter stared for a moment. Then he reached over and put his arm around the soon-to-be-departing Missy Lewis.

Guess I deserved that. I'm the one who started this dueling dates thing.

Flash glared at everyone, sitting in sullen silence and occasionally holding his arm with sad-eyed pathos.

A cloud of heavy black steam-smoke descended over the center ring and the people in the first three dozen rows.

How lucky we are that Harry was able to get such great tickets to this cultural event.

Lowered from the ceiling—in a sort of caged elevator—came a bearded, bandanna-clad man in what seemed to be full bondage gear, complete with a black leather mask and a whip. His hair seemed to be caked with egg white, and his skin glistened. A single gold tooth twinkled from his sneer. He resembled a playful medieval executioner having a bad hair day.

Mary Jane looked around for Wendy, who was three seats to her left. Leaning forward, she caught her eye. Wendy returned the stare, eyebrows raised in a silent question.

"Dibs!" Mary Jane mouthed their shorthand for whenever they saw a cute guy.

Wendy laughed, and for that instant everything seemed normal between them again.

And then the announcer's voice boomed.

"Ladies and gentlemen," he began in an exaggerated deep voice and a theatrical echo. At that point, one of the "ladies" in the audience climbed on the back of her seat and shouted "Kill 'em, Demon! Suck their eyes out!"

The crowed roared its approval. Someone spilled a beer down Mary Jane's back.

*This is going to be a very long night.*

"Tonight, we have a real treat for you folks," the announcer continued. Where was he? His voice seemed to float from above, like an invisible wrestling deity.

*If he's smart, he's calling in the announcements from his condo in Jersey.*

"Tonight, the Demon Knife Master will destroy his enemy—YOU!"

That did it. The place went nuts. The Demon Knife Master, lowered rather gently to the ring, pulled a large buzz saw from the corner and pulled the ignition.

The landscaping infomercial from hell.

Mary Jane looked up at the ceiling, hoping to find something of interest, such as a roof. But the whole arena was blanketed with fake smoke and black balloons trailing yards of black crepe paper.

The birthday decorations for Satan's youngest kid.

She looked down, again hoping for something of interest. And there was, indeed, something of interest. If she happened to collect flattened wads of old chewing gum or smashed paper cups. There were also crumpled pieces of paper with dollops of mustard, ketchup and relish—forensic evidence of hot dogs from another time.

Harry shoved her arm and pointed to the ring. A silicon-endowed woman wearing a vinyl bikini was holding up a sign.

"A thousand bucks a minute—if you dare!"

A thousand bucks a minute to be seen in that ridiculous bikini? A thousand bucks a minute to sit through this ridiculous display of stupidity?

"It's not nearly enough," she shouted to Harry.

"You're right! It's great stuff!" She could barely hear him.

Then a big door with a ten-foot high black question mark was wheeled into the center.

Yeah, I was wondering the same thing—what the hell am I doing here?

The chick in the bikini walked over to the Demon, her spike heels slightly unsteady, and kissed his cheek. He growled like one of Siegfried and Roy's big cats. Then she minced over to the door, and with great ceremony turned the knob.

Mary Jane was half expecting to see a pizza delivery guy. But it was a buff-looking man in a white tee-shirt and a gold chain with a disk the size of a hubcap. His wrists were encased in yet more gold chains, and he wore a pair of precariously tight leather pants.

Never underestimate the importance of the right accessory.

"Ladies and gentlemen," the phantom announcer called. "For one thousand dollars a minute, one of YOU—a member of our audience—has volunteered to take on THE DEMON KNIFE MASTER!"

The crowd exploded.

"I give you tonight's first challenger...THE INTIMIDATOR!"

What's he intimidated by—good taste?

The bikini produced an oversized timer. A gong was rung.

Mary Jane glanced over at Peter, who was staring at the ring with radar-like intensity.

He's actually watching this?

By the time she looked back at the ring, the

Intimidator was being carried away and the Demon Knife Master was jogging around the ring in a bizarre victory lap.

The clock was stopped at three seconds.

And again, the crowd went wild.

Please, don't tell me they think this is all real!

Mary Jane checked out her friends, all of them. And every one was cheering, all eyes on the ring.

Am I missing something?

Maybe this was like opera or water polo—an acquired taste. Perhaps she was unable to appreciate the finer points of the performance, or sport, or whatever one called wrestling. It could be that on some level, this was a satisfying and deeply moving display of humanity. Of manhood. A morality tale of good versus evil. A universal show of man allowing his primitive self to be unleashed within a secure environment.

Then a massive fart noise blasted from the speakers.

Maybe not.

One by one, the Demon Knife Master's victims were trotted out like unwitting human sacrifices. The more menacing the opponent, the more the crowd cheered. They even loved the obvious mismatches, the blood-lust taking over any sense of fair play, or even fake fair play. One poor guy looked like an accountant who wandered in by accident. He lasted less than a second.

Probably mistook this place for a karaoke bar.

Another guy wore fake fur, although to Mary Jane

it looked suspiciously like a blue bathroom mat and toilet seat cover. He came close to two seconds before being flushed.

With every defeat came the fart noise.

How much longer could this go on?

She looked over for Peter, but he was gone.

Lucky guy.

"Ladies and gentlemen! For our final challenger of the evening, we have..."

There was a rustling of paper.

"We have...The SPIDER-MAN!"

The door opened. And there stood a very average silhouette of a man in some sort of blue and red outfit. He stepped forward, and it became apparent he was wearing a leotard and stocking!

Even Mary Jane began to laugh. The guy was hooted, not booed. He didn't deserve the boos. He was beneath boos. He wore a red hood, almost a ski mask thing, tight and suffocating. With big round eyes.

The bikini did a magnificent job of swinging her hips as she set the timer. The gong was struck.

The Demon Knife Master didn't even attempt a menacing move. He pretended to trim his nails with the buzz saw.

And then, out of nowhere, the leotard guy flipped over and kicked DKM right on his cocky chin!

For the first time all evening, a hush fell over the crowd as DKM—his eyes wide in comical shock—reeled back a few steps before steadying himself.

Finally, some decent acting!

Now he looked pissed.

He lunged to the leotard guy, his one gold tooth glinting with evil. And the leotard guy jumped up and somehow landed behind DKM! Before the crowd could take in that stunt, he yanked the legs out from under the lumbering DKM.

There was mass confusion.

What was the crowd supposed to do? Cheer? Boo? Chant "Kill, kill" again?

Mary Jane rose to her feet. "Go Spider-Man!"

What did I just do?

But soon everyone was cheering the Spider-Man! The seconds ticked by like minutes: one, two, then three...

The bikini kept on glancing nervously over her shoulder, wondering what to do. Shrugging to no one in particular.

Now the Demon Knife Master was serious. And grunting. And...was that real blood?

The Spider-Man was spectacular!

Then he did a cartwheel, a flip and ended in a mid-air split. Mary Jane stopped clapping.

That's the same combo I showed Peter!

She watched his every step and leap. The spotlight was following him now.

And that looks like my leotards and tights. The ones I left over at Peter's.

Was it possible?

The gong clanged.

The Demon Knife Master was down for the count. And a guy in a black and white shirt stepped into the ring and raised the Spider-Man's arm over his head in triumph.

"And the winner, for the first time in Wrestle Cage Rage history, is the challenger! He reached the limit— five minutes! Now he is invited back next week to defend his title of Master of the Wrestle Cage Rage!"

The place erupted, and for a moment Mary Jane wondered if stomping feet and rabid shouts could actually bring an arena crumbling down.

Within a few seconds another bout began, but the crowd was still yelling for the Spider-Man.

Someone tapped her on the shoulder.

"Peter!" Mary Jane exclaimed.

He appeared cool, collected, and was carrying a tray of sodas and chips.

"The one with the bent straw is for you," he shouted. "Diet."

"Thanks. Hey, where were you?"

"Killer lines at the concession stand." He passed the food out, as Harry described what had just happened.

Peter seemed fascinated.

No way could he have been the Spider-Man. That guy was obviously hooked up to wires in the ceiling.

Anyway, it was an interesting—although preposterous—thought.

After it was all over, Harry took her home, the two piling into the back seat of the limo waiting outside the venue before she noticed Flash trailing behind them a little uncertainly. He stared at the ground while kicking a bottlecap along the sidewalk. Mare Jane tugged on Harry's jacket sleeve. "You're going to give Flash a ride, too, right?"

"Huh? Oh...sure," he said, a touch reluctantly. "Come on, bro."

Mary Jane was immensely relieved. As she slid over to the far side of the limo to make room for Flash, she realized she had been dreading being alone with Harry at the end of the night. She was beginning to feel like it had been a mistake to let him kiss her. She stared out the window as Flash played with the lit buttons on the ceiling console until Harry told him to lay off.

She had a lot to think about.

\* \* \*

Cheerleading practice took up more time than Mary Jane ever imagined it would. Every afternoon she was in the gym, clapping and stomping and smiling in unison with the other girls.

Actually, it was pretty boring.

She was beginning to wonder of she'd made a major mistake. Other than the few moments at the basketball games, when they were front and center, the world of the varsity cheerleader was vastly overrated.

Of course there were some perks. Like the guys. It seemed she had dated almost every member of the basketball team (except, of course, for Peter, the star), and now she was beginning to go through the varsity football roster.

And Harry Osborn was paying more attention than ever. It was flattering, really. But she didn't have that much to say to him. It wasn't like it was with Wendy, who always used to catch on to Mary Jane's jokes and come back with her own. It certainly wasn't like Peter.

Peter.

She only saw him a couple of times after that night at wrestling. Sure, they worked on the science project, which was due the following week. But Peter seemed to have lost interest in not only the project, but in school itself. He was cutting classes and hanging out with the cheerleaders and the cool jocks.

Sometimes Mary Jane felt as if the world had gone slightly mad.

And then something miraculous happened.

It was late one afternoon, and she was exhausted after a marathon cheerleading practice. Miss Downey had forced them to learn a brand-new routine, a brand-new lame routine. The other girls were more than cranky. They were downright bitchy, to each other, to Mary Jane. Even to Miss Downey, who decided to demonstrate her authority by making them do fifty push-ups and a hundred sit-ups while she sat on the bench, spinning her stupid whistle and chugging bottles of OZ.

Mary Jane was sore, discouraged and utterly sick of cheerleaders, little pleated skirts and Miss Adolph Hitler Downey.

"Hey, Mom," she called when she entered the apartment. As usual there was no answer. But at least Mike wasn't there.

She'd picked up the mail downstairs, rolled up into a Skye Bleu magazine (free for all of the lucky Skye Bleu salesgals). Inside were the usual bills, flyers, a delivery menu from a new Chinese restaurant.

A single letter fluttered to the linoleum. With little interest, Mary Jane picked it up.

Then she realized it was addressed to her.

And in the upper left hand corner of the envelope was a familiar embossed name.

"The Manhattan School of Ballet." Her former ballet school, the one that fed right into the company.

Perplexed, and a little nervous (had they discovered that the Watsons owed more money from old tuition?), she ripped it open.

"Dear Miss Mary Jane Watson,

"We are pleased to offer you a full scholarship to the advanced dance division of the Manhattan School of Ballet...."

Her heart flipped, then began to pound. Was this

some sort of mistake? A cruel prank?

"...came to our attention through one of the company's patrons..."

Could Granny have had something to do with this? But Granny had been in Paris for the past eight months. Maybe she called, or wrote.

"...offers classes six days a week, and you are, of course, encouraged to take full advantage of this privilege..."

An unfamiliar sense of elation ran through her like an electric current.

"Oh my God!"

Now she could quit cheerleading! Once again she would be in the world of ballet, not Ruby's House-O-Dance!

"OH MY GOD!"

She had to tell someone, anyone!

Without bothering to call, she grabbed the letter and ran over to Peter's house. Uncle Ben answered the door.

"Hello, Mary Jane!" He greeted cheerfully. "Were you supposed to meet Peter here?"

"No, no," she gasped. "But is he here?"

"I'm afraid not. He's at the gym or something. Shall I tell him you came by?"

"Yes, please! Could you tell him that..." Then she laughed, a delighted, joyful laugh, and Uncle Ben joined in.

"Must be good news!"

"It is, the best! I just got a full scholarship to the Manhattan School of Ballet!"

Uncle Ben whistled through his teeth, then—with an ear to ear grin—gave her an enormous hug. "Congratulations, sweetie! You deserve it!"

"Oh, thank you, thank you!" She hugged him back. "Please, could you just pass that on? I've got to go!"

"I sure will! Again, Mary Jane—congratulations!"

She smiled.

What a wonderful man!

Then she ran over to Wendy's house. Her mom seemed surprised to see Mary Jane, but not nearly as surprised as Wendy was.

"So what's up?" Wendy asked coolly.

"I just got a full scholarship to the Manhattan School of Ballet!"

"You're kidding."

"Nah! I can take classes every single day after school, and all day Saturday! I can't believe this! I mean, it's a dream come true!"

"Wow. Congratulations. But what about cheerleading?"

"Ah, forget it! I'd pretty much decided to quit anyway. I hate it. Hey..." Mary Jane slipped the precious letter back into her pocket. "I have an idea. How about if I teach you all of the routines? You'll be picked for sure then!"

"Really? You'd do that for me?"

"Of course I would. We'll figure out when and where later. Listen, I have to go now."

"Wow, Mary Jane. This is fantastic, really! I know how you've missed ballet."

"I have. So much I've been afraid to admit it to myself." And the moment the words were out, she knew it was true. "I have a feeling everything is going to be great from now on."

Wendy nodded. Then, a bit stiffly, and finally with real exultation, Wendy reached over and hugged her. "You go, girl!"

Suddenly Mary Jane felt like singing! With a backward wave over her shoulder, she ran to Harry's house. He'd be excited for her, too! She wasn't in the mood for anyone who didn't understand what she was feeling.

She skipped up the winding walkway, roses on either side. The Osborn place looked like a Tudor mansion mistakenly dropped in the middle of Forest Hills, Queens. There was a massive brass knocker on the door, and she half expected to see Henry VIII step over the threshold, a capon in one hand, leg of lamb in the other.

She was about to knock, when she heard an angry voice on the other side of the door.

"Goddamn it, Nelson! We need to increase the potency is what I'm saying. Understand English? Comprende?"

There was a pause as the voice, which she recognized as belonging to Harry's dad Norman Osborn, listened on the phone.

"Yeah, that Parker kid. He's been drinking it, and he's our best test case. Brat was a twerp a month ago, now he's the biggest thing to hit the athletic department since the jock strap. He's the goddamn star of the basketball team. OZ *must* be effective."

Another pause.

"Yes, of course there are side effects. It's a high performance formula. You have to take the risks in stride. But look at Parker—total squirt until he pounded a few OZ bottles... No, it's *better* than 'roid rage.' No, Harry's fine. The kid's an ox, takes after his old man," he chuckled.

"You must be joking. Addiction isn't a side effect, *it's a feature*. The kids already love the taste. No, proceed as planned. I want hard evidence of threshold levels. Up the dosage until we see some fatalities. Begin immediately. I've already got Legal working on a statement...."

All of Mary Jane's joy evaporated. Swiftly she ran as far as she could, within a few blocks of her own home. Then she walked slowly, thoughtfully.

She had to do something.

Peter. He could help. He would know what to do.

She would call him as soon as she got home. Tell him to stop drinking the OZ. And that people were watching him.

Good. Now she had a plan.

The television was blaring when she opened the door. Her mother was standing in the living room, her face bathed in blue light.

"Oh, honey," she said when she saw Mary Jane. Before she could react, her mother gave her a gentle hug. "It's horrible."

"What's horrible?" She swallowed. "What's going on?"

Then Mary Jane looked at the screen.

It was Peter's house!

There was yellow police tape wound around the two front columns of the front porch, the exact place she had been standing just a few hours earlier. Flashing red and yellow lights blinked as a uniformed cop and an official-looking man in a suit bent over a large pool of blood on the wooden plank porch.

"To recap the breaking news," the anchorwoman read in solemn tones. "An apparent robbery attempt has resulted in the shooting death of Benjamin Parker..."

"No!" Mary Jane cried. She felt the room shift around her, and suddenly felt like she was under water.

"...no witnesses. His wife and nephew discovered the body..."

"I have to go over there."

"Mary Jane, no, don't!" Madeline Watson exclaimed. "Don't go. There are horrible sights—the body may even be there still. Please, honey. Don't go."

Mary Jane had already turned to leave.

\* \* \*

The jog over to Peter's house was a dull haze. Nothing was focused; the only thing that mattered was getting there. Seeing Peter.

The instant she turned the corner she saw the police cars, one rammed up on the lawn. An ambulance with the back door swinging open. The neighbors were craning to catch a glimpse of...of what? Of a nice man who had been killed? Of a spot of blood?

"Okay, folks, stay back. All of you. Go on home. There's nothing to see. Show's over."

Mary Jane started towards the porch.

"Hey, Miss. Stop right there."

"Officer, I'm a friend of the family's. Please."

"Yeah, yeah. So is everyone." He waved a flashlight. "Move on. This is a crime scene, a restricted zone..."

And then she heard it. The most terrible sound she had ever heard.

It came from the side of the house, from the driveway. It was a low, wracking sob.

It was Peter.

He was on the ground, hunched over, all alone.

She ran to him and she, too, knelt on the ground.

"Peter," she whispered, placing her arm over his shoulder.

He stiffened. Then he turned towards her.

"It's all my fault." His voice was broken, ragged.

"No, no," she felt his tears, hot and wet, on her hands. And she, too, began to cry.

"Oh, Mary," he turned his face towards her shoulder, his entire body heaving.

She held him fiercely, protectively. And a single thought consumed her.

Never again would she allow anyone to hurt Peter Parker.

Never again.

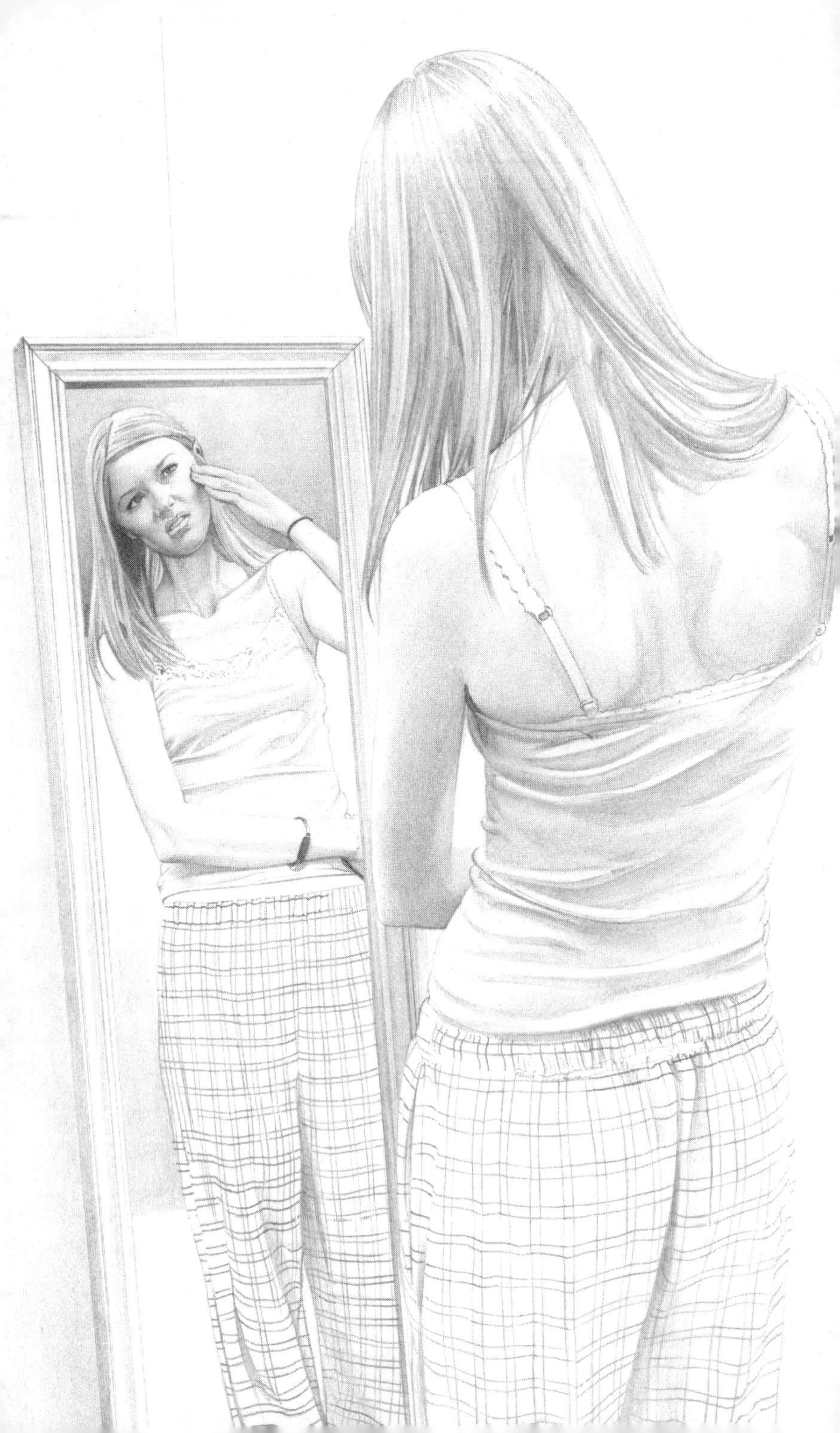

# chapter 7

Mary Jane's first thought upon waking was that it had all been a dream.

Flashes of the previous day replayed in her mind. The moment she opened the letter from the Manhattan School of Ballet, the sense of unexpected, soaring elation that rushed through her. Then running over to Peter's—the twinkle on Uncle Ben's craggy features when she told him of her scholarship. The scent of his aftershave, an old man's mixture of witch hazel and something vaguely musky. The reluctant, then genuine smile from Wendy.

Then it all became a surrealistic nightmare, like a student film shot with an unsteady camera. The bizarre, shouted half-conversation she overheard at the Osborns'. The peculiar spinning in the pit of her stomach, accentuating the perpetual feeling of nausea she'd been battling the past few weeks.

And then the news of Uncle Ben's murder, the sounds of Peter sobbing.

Would she ever be able to erase those heartbroken sobs from her memory?

Twisting a feather pillow, she was unable to push those visions away. The delirious joy of the ballet scholarship followed by the sickening spiral of that evening.

The door to her bedroom opened slowly. "Mary Jane?"

She hugged her pillow tighter and pretended to be asleep. The last thing she needed was a chat with her well-meaning mother.

"Mary Jane? Honey, it's time to wake up for school."

Go away, just go away.

"Five minutes," her mother whispered. She paused for a few moments. Mary Jane could feel her stare from across the room, watching for telltale signs of whatever teen disorder du-jour she had read about in last week's supermarket tabloid.

Did the *National Inquisitor* cover "What to do when your daughter's world falls apart" next to its penetrating investigation of alien poodles?

Her mother sighed heavily, and finally the door closed.

Slowly Mary Jane sat up, swinging her legs over the edge of the bed and tapping her feet to locate her slippers, still sleepy. Still numb with the shock of last night.

She was tired, so tired, just as she had been for the past few weeks. It was hard to get through the day, much less do her best at cheerleading or keep awake in class. Even going up and down the school steps was tiring.

Then she caught a glimpse of herself in the full-length mirror on the closet door.

My God, who is that skank?

Reflected back was the image of a painfully thin, pasty girl with stick-like legs dangling from beneath an oversized tee-shirt. Her hair was lank, lifeless—like the "before" picture in a conditioner advertisement. But it was her eyes, dull and ringed with brown circles, which startled her the most. Gone was the face she had taken for granted, the features described as pretty and vivacious. In its place was the vacant look of someone who had been ill for a long time. It was the face of suffering.

How could just a few pounds make such a difference? All she'd wanted was to make herself better, more attractive. More like those girls on the covers of magazines, or in music videos. In her mind she thought she had managed to achieve that goal. She'd felt triumphant, in control, and above all more beautiful than she had ever been.

Yet now, from across the room, reflected in the undeniable truth on the form of a full-length mirror from Joe's Dollar Store, was the reality of what she had become.

She wasn't a babe, or model-thin, or stylishly slender. This wasn't an image to be desired. Instead she looked like a lollipop stick figure. One of those famine-stricken waifs from Third-World countries you could sponsor in those infomercials mocked by her mother's boyfriend.

Slowly she raised her hand to her cheek, lightly touching the newly protruding bones, the hollow temples.

How the hell can I help anyone in this shape? No wonder I haven't been able to think clearly. Why didn't anyone tell me I look like crap?

But someone did. Peter.

*"They call you 'Rex,' MJ. Short for anorexia."*

This was madness. Her self-designed diet had been starvation, not a clever self-improvement project. That's why she hadn't felt well, been unable to think clearly. Why her mind wandered, her emotions rollercoastered.

But that had to stop. Now. She needed to regain control, not next week or tomorrow but now.

Still shaky, she stood up, waiting for the head-rush to subside, and padded into the kitchen. Her mother was at the table, a piece of dry toast in one hand and a mug of black coffee—no sugar, no cream—in the other.

"Mary Jane!"

"Hi, Mom," she went over to the fridge. "Do we have any eggs?"

"Of course," she put down the toast and coffee. "For your science project or something?"

"Nah. For breakfast or something."

"Oh. Want me to make you some scrambled eggs?"

"No thanks. I can manage."

Her mother stared in confusion before placing her empty mug—with a puckered lipstick ring on the rim—in the sink.

Alone in the kitchen, Mary Jane made a breakfast of

eggs and whole-wheat toast. Then she sat at the table, contemplating the plate before her. She hadn't eaten this much food in an entire day, much less in a single meal, for weeks.

Slowly, she began to eat, chewing with careful deliberation. It was difficult, laborious work, battling the urge to push the plate away and run to the bathroom. Trying to erase the image in her mind of some enormously obese alter-self she would become if she consumed this much food.

Has it become this bad, that I can't eat breakfast like a normal person?

After the first few forkfuls, she stopped to rest. She would finish. She had no choice. She would become strong again. For Peter. For Wendy. For her mother. For whoever was being harmed by the stuff Norman Osborn had put in OZ.

But most of all, she would become strong again for herself.

*    *    *

At school, the hot topic was, of course, the murder of Ben Parker.

The hallways had become an instant, if unreliable, news service. Every tidbit of information, no matter how dubious the source, was worthy of serious consideration, repetition, and, of course, elaboration.

"I hear he was some sort of scientist," someone enthused. "I think he was working on some major government project, and a bunch of foreign spies wanted to silence him."

"Really? I read in the paper that they thought it was drug-related. Maybe he was head of some big South American drug cartel."

"Nah, you guys are so off base! He probably had a girlfriend with a jealous husband. Yeah, that was it. A crime of passion. Maybe the girlfriend herself popped him. I mean, they say ninety percent of murders are committed by a friend or relative of the victim. And that's a fact. I heard it on *Maury*."

"It's ninety-five percent. And it was on *Jerry Springer*."

"Hey, Peter should go on that show with the guy who talks to the dead and find out what his uncle has to say. Wouldn't that be awesome?"

It took a supreme effort not to tell them all to shut up, that they didn't know what they were talking about. But doing that wouldn't accomplish anything. Instead Mary Jane did her best to ignore the absurd comments.

She glanced around the corridors, peeked into his homeroom, but Peter was nowhere to be seen. Of course he wouldn't be at school today. How could he? His uncle was just murdered. Still, she'd been hoping to see him, to see how he was doing. To reassure herself that he was able to stand and talk and be almost normal in spite of the horror of last night.

Even through her thoughts of Peter and the thick haze of speculation about his uncle, it was impossible to ignore the weird behavior of some of the athletes or the kids coming from first period gym class.

How could she have missed this before? There was a strange aggressiveness in the air. Movements were hurried, laughter was loud. It was the artificially hyped-up atmosphere that usually occurred right before a big game or homecoming. But this was just a normal morning—albeit a normal morning following the shocking news of Ben Parker's murder.

But that was not the cause of the bizarre atmosphere. And when she scrutinized the behavior of some of the other kids, the ones who were pushing through the halls and kicking the lockers, she saw a common denominator.

All of the most aggressive behavior was coming from kids with tongues dyed either bright blue or orange. They had just consumed OZ.

Something in that sports drink was altering their personalities, maybe giving them a rush of strength. Kids fresh from gym, with hair wet and spiky from showers, stalked the halls, laughing loudly and elbowing other students out of the way.

A trio of cheerleaders passed by, not even glancing at her. One gave the girl in the center a mighty whack on the back, the misplaced friendly aggression of a grizzly bear. Instead of stumbling forward or bursting out in feminine tears, the whacked girl gave a loud, deep Jabba-the-Hut laugh.

Mary Jane blinked in shock. Wasn't that the same girl who had to sit out volleyball in gym because of an inflamed hangnail?

And were those girls' necks always as thick as Michelin tires?

Still staring at them, her attention was suddenly distracted when Howard from her math class passed by, an orange clown-like smile on his face. Instead of hugging his books and looking down at the floor as he usually did, he winked at her, a broad, comical squint of the entire left side of his face.

And then he pinched her butt.

"Howard!!"

He clicked his tongue and whistled through his teeth. "I'd like a handful of that action, babe!"

Even the kids who seemed more normal were affected by the wilding of the OZ drinkers. It was impossible not to react to such dramatic actions. The more timid students ducked when full soda cans were tossed in the classrooms. The others grabbed the cans, crushed them, and threw them back.

The teachers made vague, ineffectual attempts at quieting the kids, but they themselves were intimidated by the testosterone that seemed to be floating in the air.

Although everyone was affected, no one was saying anything. There was a conspiracy of silent acceptance, as if everyone was afraid, but even more afraid of talking about what was happening.

Even the varsity athletes were different, although it was harder to detect the changes in most of them. They were the same cocky, boisterous masters-of-their-universe they had always been. Only now they were even more so, as if they had all been turned into terminators. They were aggressive enough without any enhancements.

But now they were swaggering down the halls, elbowing others out of the way. Laughing loudly, making rude comments about other kids. In short, they acted like the gang members in a badly performed dinner theater production of *West Side Story*. They were over-the-top, finger-snapping punks.

Mary Jane shook her head in wonderment. Hadn't their parents noticed the difference? The teachers? Or were the changes universally blown off as typical teenage behavior?

Tiffany Reed passed right by, a slight girl best known for her allergies to virtually every known food group and a pathological fear of hamsters. She had so many silver medical emergency bracelets, her arm looked like a Slinky.

But today she was bracelet-free and eating—was it possible?—a bag of peanuts. It was Tiffany's mother who was largely responsible for trying to ban peanut butter from the lunchroom. How could she be munching peanuts, shell and all? Good God...make that bag and all.

And when did Tiffany grow an Adam's apple and peach fuzz?

Harry Osborn turned the corner. "Hey, babe," he whispered to Mary Jane in a husky, satin-sheet voice.

Was he any different? That was hard to tell. She took a critical look at him. He was still mad-handsome. Still dressed like a GQ cover. Yet there was something different, something that hadn't been there before.

"Harry, have you been working out?"

He grinned. "No. But I'm glad you notice my body. I sure notice yours."

Again, hard to tell with Harry.

Then it came to her. The way to find out what was happening with Norman Osborn's formula was to get closer to Norman Osborn's son. Of course! If she could get into his house, maybe do a little snooping around....

"Harry," Mary Jane cooed. It felt strange. She hadn't cooed in years. The last time had been at a puppy. "What are you doing after school?"

His eyelids were half-closed. "Maybe you could give me some ideas."

It took her a second to catch on. Was he serious? Instead of looking sexy, he looked like a dope fiend. She didn't have time to weigh the pros and cons. "How about if I come over after school?" She tried to match his seductive tone with an equally stoned voice. She twirled her hair around a finger for effect, hoping she wasn't laying it on too thick.

"Great," he said, and touched her face lightly. "I'll pick you up after cheerleading practice. I've got the car today."

With a jolt she realized she still had to break the news to Miss Downey. "Nah, I'll skip it."

"I'm flattered. Meet me by the flagpole." He winked, an expression disconcertingly similar to the one Howard from math class offered a few minutes earlier.

"By the flagpole? Nice symbolism, Freud. I'll be the one with the cigar." She ran a finger along his arm. It felt as if it had been honed, not toned.

His flawless brow wrinkled for a brief moment, then mercifully smoothed. "I didn't know you smoked cigars. Whatever. Well, see you then."

The bell rang, and the dash to class began. Nothing seemed terribly out of place then, other than the fact that the glazed brick hallways suddenly turned into the running of the bulls at Pamplona. It had always been a chaotic time when the bell rang. But she had never felt an urge to run ahead of the pack to escape being gored before.

Weird!

* * *

After a quick lunch of an apple, a turkey and cheese sandwich and milk (her inner voice screaming, "Cheese! Do you know how many calories and grams of fat are in a slice of Swiss?"), Mary Jane tapped on Miss Downey's door.

"Come in," growled a masculine voice. Was Coach Renny in there? Or Mookie, the push-broom guy?

But it was just Miss Downey seated at her desk. She took a big slurp out of a bottle marked OZ.

"Oh, Mary Jane," she put down the bottle. "I'm glad you stopped by. I've been thinking of adding a rolling tumble dismount to the pyramid and..."

"Miss Downey, I just came to tell you I'm quitting the team. I'm sorry, but you see I've..."

"You're WHAT?" Disbelief echoed off the metal file cabinets.

"I'm afraid I have to quit the team. You see, I..."

Slowly, Miss Downey rose to her feet. Suddenly she looked very tall, and very threatening. "You cannot quit the team."

Of all the responses Mary Jane had imagined, this was definitely not in the running. Gentle cajoling, perhaps. Mild disappointment, maybe. But not scarcely contained fury.

"Really, Miss Downey. I'm the newest one on the team, so I barely know the routines anyway. I lack enthusiasm. I'm just not the best choice."

"That is my decision." It was spoken in the tone of a cheerleader Gestapo. Mary Jane half expected her to click her heels. "I selected you. This is an honor. You are new here, so you cannot possibly understand the importance of the position."

"Really, Miss Downey. I understand. Really, I do. It's just that I have been offered a ballet scholarship and..."

"From whom?" Miss Downey leaned over the desk, her metal whistle clanking against a clipboard. "I can have it taken away!"

Mary Jane blinked in astonishment. Was this a joke? A sudden urge to laugh overtook her, and she clamped her hand over her mouth so Miss Downey wouldn't see.

"Yes! I can, and I will!"

"Miss Downey, this is the cheerleading squad, not the firing squad. It is a volunteer afterschool activity, like the chess club or the debating team."

"Is that what you're trying to tell me?" She cocked an eyebrow. "You are leaving cheerleading for debate and chess?"

Is she speaking with a German accent?

"No. I'm going to concentrate on ballet." She spoke slowly, carefully, as if talking someone off a ledge. "I enjoy cheerleading. But I'm better at ballet."

"Ha! Ballet. That is nothing."

"Perhaps, Miss Downey. But..."

"Nothing!" Her mouth opened so wide, Mary Jane could count the fillings.

"Well, thank you for the advice." She backed away slowly.

This probably isn't the best time to mention that Wendy would make a fabulous replacement.

"Ballet is nothing, nothing!" Then she threw back her head...and laughed. It wasn't a normal laugh. It was a Boris Karloff chuckle. It was sinister. It was diabolical.

And it was coming from the mouth of the cheer-leading coach.

"Thank you, Miss Downey," she said as she slid out of the office. "Oh, and you might want to cut down on the OZ."

But Miss Downey didn't hear a word.

As she left, Mary Jane could hear the laughter waft down the hallway.

A pale, scrawny freshman boy in oversized gym shorts stepped out of the boy's room, heard the cackling, and hopped back into the bathroom.

"Good thinking," Mary Jane called.

She was beginning to feel like she'd stepped into a Stephen King novel.

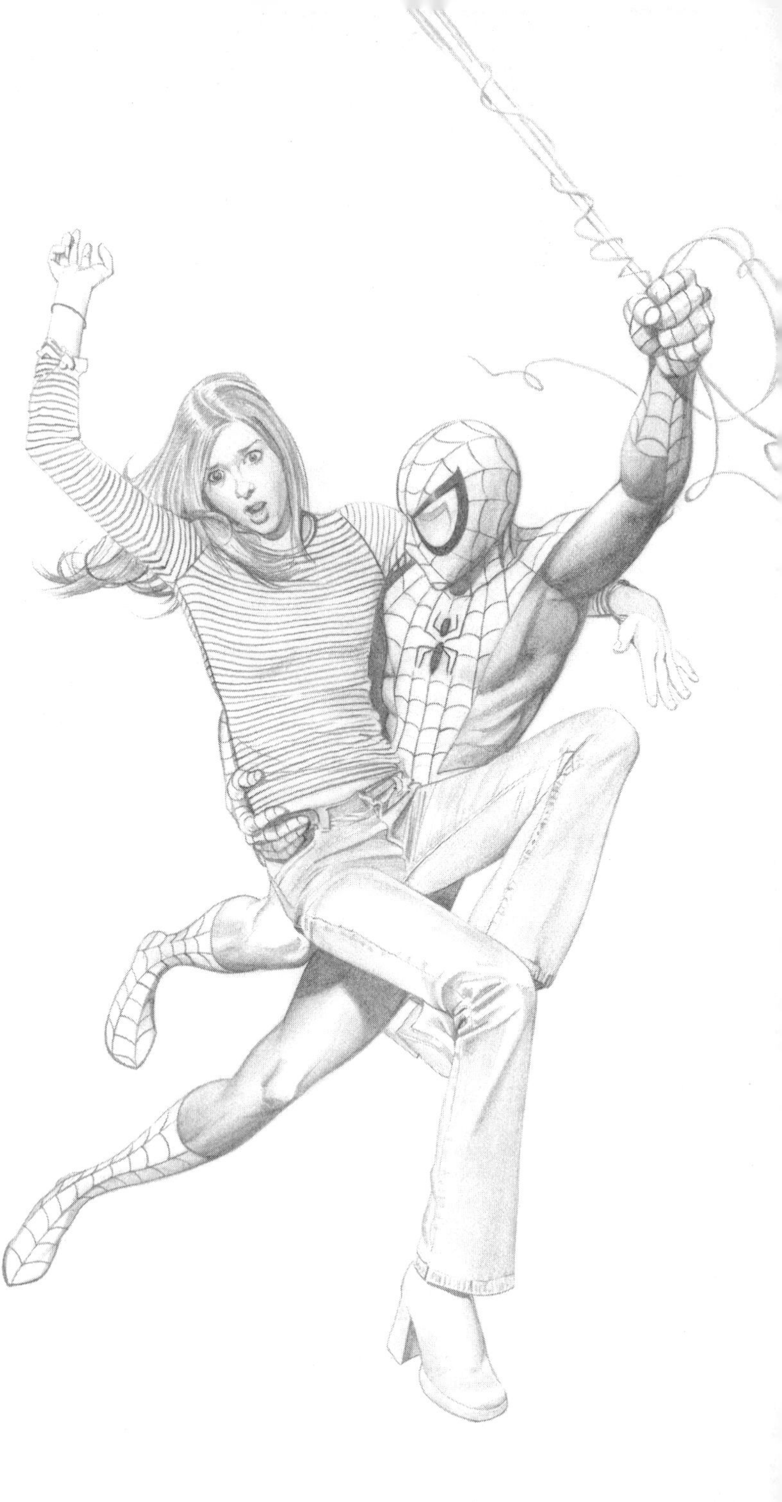

# chapter 8

Mary Jane Watson was not just the only sane person at school that day. She was also the only student who didn't have a cell phone.

There was one payphone in the entire high school, and that was just off the lobby and usually out of order.

"Must be my lucky day," she mumbled to herself when she picked up the gummy receiver and heard a faint dial tone. With that she slipped in a quarter and called Peter.

This was the third time she'd tried to get through to him that day, both other times from Wendy's cell. The line had been busy both tries. But this time she got through.

It was picked up after the seventh ring. "Hello." The voice on the other end was empty, devoid of emotion.

"Peter?"

"MJ." There was a tone of relief.

"How are you?" Stupid question.

"Swell. Couldn't be better."

"Oh, Peter, I'm so sorry. I don't know what to say."

"I know, MJ, I know." He took a deep breath, and

she could imagine his face, the phone cradled next to his ear. His eyes staring off into space. "Um, anything going on at school?"

"Yeah. Yeah, as a matter of fact there is. Listen, Peter, I hate to bother you with this, but..."

On the other end she heard the doorbell ring and the sound of hushed conversation. More neighbors, no doubt.

"Mrs. Johnson just brought over her sweet and sour liver soufflé," he said, the vague hint of a wan smile in his voice.

"Could you save me some?"

"Sure. What were you saying?"

"Peter, weird things have been going on at school. I'm sorry to bug you with this at such a time, but people have been behaving very strangely."

"I hadn't noticed."

She couldn't tell if he was just speaking automatically, or if he really hadn't noticed.

"I think there's something in that OZ stuff. You know, the sports drink."

"Yeah, I know. OZ."

"I overheard Mr. Osborn yesterday. There's a performance enhancer in it. And Peter, he mentioned your name. I think that's why you suddenly got so good at basketball."

"Yeah. Maybe."

The mechanical voice of an operator cut in, warning

her she had a minute before being cut off unless she inserted another quarter. Fumbling for change, she slipped in three dimes.

"Peter? Peter, are you still there?"

"I'm here."

"I just thought you should know. I mean, about OZ and all. Maybe you should stop drinking it, at least for the time being. I'm meeting Harry after school to see if I can find out anything."

"You're meeting Harry?" His voice took on a different edge.

"Yep. I'm hoping to find out more about what's going on."

"You're meeting Harry?"

"That's what I just said. So I was wondering if..."

In the background the doorbell rang again.

"Listen, Mary Jane. I've got to go now. Have fun with Harry."

"No, please! Don't hang up. I'm out of quarters and..."

"Bye."

"Peter, I've got to tell you something!"

There was a pause. "I'm listening."

Suddenly she felt incredibly stupid. And insensitive. What the hell did he care about what was going on at school? His uncle—no, the man who had been his father for all those years—had been brutally murdered on their front porch.

And she called to discuss a fruit drink.

"Oh, Peter." She swallowed, tears welling in her eyes. With a fingernail she began to peel a skateboard sticker off the side of the phone. "I'm so sorry."

"I know, MJ, and thank you."

"Could you give my love to Aunt May?"

"Yeah, sure."

"Okay. Well, I'll call you later."

"Thanks. Bye."

And then he was gone.

She sniffed a few times, looking at the silent, black box of a telephone.

Whatever else happened that afternoon, she was only sure of one thing. She was completely on her own.

* * *

Harry Osborn was waiting for her at the flagpole, his jacket slung over his right shoulder, the image of self-conscious cool.

"Hey, babe," he murmured.

"Hey there, Tiger." She tried not to gag on the words.

He smiled a lazy grin. "Should we go straight back to my crib?"

"Sure thing." She resisted the urge to laugh out loud.

You mean your father's crib, Harry.

His eyes brightened. "Ya know, no one else is home now. Muriel has the day off."

"Muriel?"

"The maid."

"Oh, right. The maid."

"So we'll be all alone."

"That sounds wonderful." She tried to purr, lowering her voice. But instead she just sounded butch—like every other girl at school who'd been drinking OZ.

"Okay," he pulled out his car keys and tossed them casually in the air. The cool factor was somewhat diminished when the keys slipped past his hand and landed perilously close to a pile of dog doo. He bent over, rear end pressed against the flag pole, gingerly removing the keys. Then he stood up, sniffing the key chain once to be certain it hadn't touched the poop. "But don't say I didn't warn you."

Are we going to talk like bad B-movie actors all afternoon?

"Okay, Big Boy. I'll consider myself warned." Guess so.

Harry put the top down on his car. It was so foreign, she'd never heard of the make. How many cars did this kid have?

He drove slowly, the car jerking as he shifted. "Damn thing," he muttered.

She was pretty certain the damn car was damn fine. Harry just didn't have the damn stick shift thing down pat yet.

"So, how was your day?" His head snapped as the car stalled.

"Oh, fi-fine," she tried to flip back her hair enticingly, but slapped herself in the face when he shifted. "So, when did you get your license?"

"I didn't, yet. But I've got my learner's permit," he said. The car quacked like a duck and ground to a halt. Harry swore and pounded the steering wheel. "Gotta get this thing into the shop pronto."

They eventually made it to the Osborn mansion, but not before stalling a half dozen times, causing several cars to veer off the road, and being jeered at by everyone from the mailman to a bunch of ten year-olds on push scooters.

"Well," he said, rubbing his neck. "Here we are."

"Yes indeed. Here we are."

Really, someone should jot down these witty remarks before they are lost forever.

The heavily carved oak door opened with an ominous creak, and he held his arm out to usher her in.

The interior of the house was stunning, in a deliberate, self-conscious way. It was clearly designed with impact, not comfort, in mind. MJ knew these kinds of houses. The magnificent expanses of wood, gleaming corridors of marble. Priceless carpets, rare antiques and custom-designed pieces. Oil paintings by artists with works in the Whitney and the Met.

All of this reminded her of the kids from Park Avenue. Of all those penthouses, the gleaming duplexes.

Those kids and those years felt very far away now. So strange to be back in grand surroundings. It made her vaguely uncomfortable.

Even their own home had been somewhat like this once, although not quite as opulent. Back when their family had been whole, before her father left for who knows where. She swallowed a dull ache in her chest. That was a long time ago.

Focus, MJ. Remember why you're here.

"So," Harry smiled. "Would you like a drink?"

"Sure," she smiled back, a little too brightly. "What do you have?"

"How about the house drink, OZ?"

Great. Hormonal changes and fluorescent tongues. What an attractive combination.

"Um, how about..." what should she go for? Diet soda? Orange juice? Nah. Something as pretentious as the surroundings. "How about an imported mineral water? Oh, and I only drink the kind from France. With the little bubbles."

He smiled. "Sure! I'll see what we have."

He led her through the spotless foyer into a football field-sized living room that was paneled entirely in dark, polished wood, with stained-glass lamps looming overhead. A brown sectional sofa covered in buttery leather snaked through the center of the room. On the far side was a long mahogany bar, like something out of a turn-of-the-century men's club. MJ scanned the room while Harry rummaged through a wood-covered refrigerator that was disguised to look like a fancy cabinet. There was another entrance to the room, and it looked like it led to a home office. From where she was standing, Mary Jane could see a desk and computer through the entryway.

"Uh, is this the stuff?" He squinted at a green bottle.

"Sure, I guess so."

He nodded, then began searching for a wine glass. With a shrug he opened the freezer section and pulled out a couple of frosted beer steins. He filled them both, emptying the bottle.

"Here we go." He handed her the mug, and they toasted each other.

"Cheers," she smiled. "Why don't you sit here, next to me?" She patted the sofa, noting a large stack of folders and papers piled on an end table about two feet away. He wasted no time in jumping to her side.

"Soooo," he began. Then he chugged the whole mug of sparkling water before belching. Proud of himself, he gestured towards her own full-mug. "Slam it!"

It seemed the only way to entertain Harry was to join in a burping contest.

Slowly, she sipped.

"You can do better than that!"

She had to get him distracted, to leave her alone for long enough for some serious snooping. So she gulped half the mug. "This water tastes a little funny. Might be the vintage," she said in what she hoped was an authoritative tone. "Harry, what I'm really in the mood for is some root beer. Do you have any?"

"I think so. I'll go down to the basement and see if we have some in storage."

"Great!"

He bounded from the room, and she heard his steps fading, then the sound of the basement door opening.

Immediately she put down the drink and turned to the papers on the end table. Maybe there would be something there...anything that might help explain what was in OZ. There were letters to the company that maintained the lawn, a series of memos on staff changes. Some guy named Bob McKenna was being fired in Marketing. "Poor Bob," she whispered.

Then she heard Harry coming back. "Good news! I found a whole case of root beer! This is my father's favorite kind. It's from Ohio, I think." The bottles rattled as he carried a large wooden case.

One quick look at the other stack and she leapt back to the couch.

"Did I say root beer?" She blinked innocently. "I'm sorry, what I meant to say was orange soda."

"Orange soda?" His shoulder's slumped and he put down the bottles with a small grunt.

MJ crossed the room and ran her hand over his left bicep. "Wow, check out the muscles on you." He flushed, then flexed happily for her. "Ooh...nice. Harry,

I really *love* orange soda. Ple-ase?" She drew out the word, squeezing his arm slowly.

"Okay, I'll check. Might take me a while though."

"Take as much time as you need."

He smiled slowly. "Great! Be right back."

This time she made it into Norman Osborn's home office. Besides the expansive walnut desk and computer, there was a fax machine and a small photocopier. There were also two filing cabinets. The first one was locked. She pulled on the top drawer of the second one, and it slid open easily. Skimming the tabs, she realized nothing confidential would be in there. She needed to get into the locked cabinet. She eased the drawer shut and rushed back into the living room when she heard Harry's steps.

"Hey, what are you doing?" He snapped open a bottle of orange soda.

"I was just looking for the bathroom."

"Ah, it's over there."

"Yeah, thanks. I found it." When he reached for another bottle, she studied some of the paintings mounted on the walls. Maybe one of them concealed a wall safe?

"Harry, I'm starving," she sighed.

"You're kidding? Why didn't you say anything when we drove past the burger place?"

"I wasn't hungry then. I am now. Can you get me something?"

"I guess so." He seemed peeved. "Like what?"

"Maybe some celery. Cut in little two-inch sticks."

"Sure. Come into the kitchen with me."

"I could, but, Harry..." MJ paused, wondering what she could possibly say to convince him. "I think it's really sexy when guys aren't afraid to show they know their way around a kitchen. It's so...progressive," she finished a bit lamely.

He stood for a moment. "Really?"

"Definitely. It's really hot." Mary Jane wondered if she'd finally gone overboard.

Then Harry shrugged. "If you say so." If he wasn't exactly gracious, at least he left the room.

In a flash she was back in Osborn's office, peeking behind paintings and checking for a wall safe. No luck. He'd be back soon from the kitchen. She had to...

And then she saw it, just behind a statue of some Greek god. A small, box-like safe.

"You want some ranch dressing or something?" Harry called.

"Sounds great!"

How was she possibly going to get into this thing? Would Harry know the combination? She heard him whistling, and ran back to the couch.

"Hey," Harry winked as he rounded the corner with a huge tray, his voice lowered several octaves.

Ya ought to take that act to Vegas, Harry. You'd kill 'em there.

She sat on the sofa and snuggled up next to a big pillow. "Hey."

He slid next to her on the sofa, filling his mug with soda, then topping off hers. "This stuff is from Canada. My dad says it's really expensive."

"It's nice," she sipped it. "Very orange-y."

She could hear the tick of the wall clock.

God, I have absolutely nothing to say to this guy!

Then she had a sudden flash of inspiration. She dropped her head, letting a curtain of red hair hide half her face from view. "Oh, Harry. I'm really bummed out."

He swallowed his mug in a single gulp, then let a deeply resonant belch rip. "Why? Not enough celery?"

"No, no. That's fine. It's just that, well..."

"Your skin sure is soft-looking." He touched her cheek. "Feels soft, too."

"Thanks. I use lotion. Anyway, I'm really sad. It's about the science project."

"The science project?"

"Yeah," she made a pouty-face. "Peter and I are analyzing OZ."

"You are? Damn, wish I had thought of that! I could just get the formula from my dad."

"I wish I could do that. I'm having a terrible time figuring out what's in it."

Then he put down the mug. "You know, you're really hot."

"If I only had that project finished, I could think of other things. Like you. Like us."

He stared at her, his mouth slack. Then he smiled. "You're much hotter than Missy Lewis." He put his arm around her shoulders.

"Um, thanks. You're hot, too. It's just that..." With determination she pulled away from him.

"What's wrong?"

"I'm just too distracted to think of anything else other than the project. If I get a bad grade, my mom's going to kill me. For real."

"Well..." he began, his hand creeping up onto her knee. "I guess I could give you the formula from my dad's office. But it has to be top secret, you know. He'd kill me if he found out I even know where he keeps it."

"Where is that?"

Harry grinned. "With his stash of Italian porn. That's how I found it."

"Oh, Harry. I'd be so grateful. Could you get it now?"

He hesitated just a moment, then he jumped up and went back into his dad's office. In a few minutes he returned with the papers in hand, his face a bit flushed. "Here. I made you a copy."

"You're the best!" He handed it to her, and she stuffed it into her backpack.

Without warning, he leaned over and kissed her. It was a big, sloppy, wet, awful kiss.

Gently she pushed him away. "No, Harry."

"Aw, come on," he protested. "You said so yourself. Now that the science project is in the bag, you can think about us." His voice cracked. "I've been waiting for this since the other day in the limo."

She stared at him and realized she'd played her role all too well. A moment of panic jolted through her. Then another feeling took its place. Guilt.

What the hell am I doing?

He put his arm around her waist and pulled her in tight.

How am I going to get myself out of this?

Mary Jane took a deep breath as he pressed himself against her. She mustered all of her skills.

And belched as loudly as she could.

"Whoa, gnarly!" He smiled with approval.

"Harry, I don't feel well. I think I might throw up."

"Nah. Come on, quit playing games..."

"How old is that ranch dressing?"

"Huh?"

"The ranch dressing?"

"I dunno. But you didn't have any."

"Yes I did. I had lots when you were in your dad's office."

That didn't stop him.

"Harry, please!" This was getting out of control.

The "please" had no effect. It suddenly felt like Harry had eight hands. One slid up her ribcage towards her chest and touched off some kind of inner switch. Cold anger kicked in. That was it.

Her knee jerked up between his legs almost before she realized what she was doing.

Harry crumpled on the carpet, with a yelp, clutching himself and moaning. "Awww!" His voice was high, almost pitiful as he rolled back and forth. "Help!"

She stared at him, stricken. Trying to think of something to do, to say. She really hadn't meant to knee him that hard. It just happened. "Harry, I'm so sorry. Are you okay? Can I do anything?"

"I think you've done enough," he groaned with a mix of pain and what sounded like shame.

"Can I..." Mary Jane felt awful. She was not just a tease, she was a bully.

"Just go, MJ."

She grabbed her backpack, blurted another "sorry" at the boy on the floor, and fled.

Her eyes burning, Mary Jane ran from the house. She sprinted across a busy intersection, barely stopping to glance both ways. She didn't notice the grey sedan speeding up to catch a yellow light until she heard the horn blaring and a red figure streaked into her peripheral vision. She felt herself lifted into the air and suddenly found herself on the other side of the street in the company of...

It was the Spider-Man!

"Are you okay?" His voice was muffled beneath the mask, but he sounded anxious.

"I guess so, I wasn't paying attention." She took deep breaths, trying to get her heart to stop pounding.

"You should be more careful. Where were you

181

running from? Your boyfriend's house?"

"He's not my..." Mary Jane stared at him. Something about his voice. It was so warm. And oddly familiar.

"I saw you run out of that big house over there. I thought I heard someone ask for help in there. Did he...?" His face was obscured by the mask. This outfit looked a little different than the one he was wearing the other day—it was sleek and smooth, nothing like her old leotard and tights.

"No, don't worry. I'm fine," she said. Mary Jane could tell he was studying her through the opaque panels over his eyes. She smoothed her hair down self-consciously, thinking she must look like a mess.

The Spider-Man cleared his throat. "Do you need help getting home?"

"No," she looked at the mask, trying to make out his features. But it was impossible to tell who he was, what he looked like. "Really, I'm okay."

That voice. She knew that voice.

"Is that you, Peter?"

He made a sound. Laughter, maybe? A strange, gruff sound. Then he shook his head. "Just call me Spider-Man."

"Yeah, sure. Then you can call me Wonder Woman."

He made that noise again, but it was impossible to tell his expression. "I'll take you home."

"No. Really, no. I'm not going home yet."

"Where are you going? Out dancing?"

"No. I have to stop by to see a friend."

The Q-65A Bus turned the corner, and she raised her hand to flag it down. This would get her to Peter's house in just a few minutes.

*If I get there, and Peter's not home, I'll know for sure that Spider-Man's really Peter!*

In spite of everything that had just happened, she smiled. "Thank you."

"Hey, it's nothing. Just your friendly neighborhood Spider-Man."

She boarded the bus, the driver gaped at the guy in the blue and red costume. "What the hell?"

"Don't worry, he's not getting on." She turned back, but he was already gone. "Bye!"

Whoever he was, this guy in tights, she was certain of one thing: Something about him was incredibly hot!

* * *

It took her even less time than she thought to get to the Parkers' home. Cars were parked out front, and bits of yellow police tape were still attached to the porch, flapping gently in the wind, benign as springtime laundry. But it wasn't springtime laundry. It was hideous yellow tape proclaiming that a murder had taken place. Someone had cleaned off the blood stains, and there was an incongruous scent of pine cleaner and a few splashes of water on the front walk.

Who'd had to clean it up?

Peter.

Her stomach lurched at that thought. Of course it would be Peter. He'd never let Aunt May swab her own husband's blood.

She rang the doorbell. Shadowy figures could be seen through the closed curtains, the murmur of hushed voices and tisking and exclamations of "what a shame, a shock" in subdued undertones.

An elderly man in a blue suit answered the door. "Yes?"

"Um, hi. I'm a friend of Peter's. I know he probably isn't here but..."

The man smiled. "He's upstairs in his room."

Wanna bet on that?

He held the door open for her to enter. Everyone was wearing dark colors, eating cookies and sipping tea. In a corner chair sat Mrs. Parker, looking old and stunned and slightly confused. People were around her, but no one seemed to be talking to her. She stared at Mary Jane for a moment, slightly confused. Then she smiled.

"Mary Jane, my dear."

She rushed to her side. "Oh, Aunt May, I'm so sorry."

"I know, dear. I know. I'm so glad you're here. Peter's been in his room all day, hardly coming out at all. I'm so worried about him, Mary Jane. This has brought it all back again, his parents, the crash. No child should have to go through that once, much less twice."

"He's stronger than he looks," she whispered.

"Oh, I know that. But he takes things to heart. He thinks this was all his fault, somehow he blames himself. See if you can talk some sense into him."

"I'll try." Aunt May patted her cheek, and she turned to go up to Peter's room.

"And see if you can get him to eat something," she said, as someone offered her a cup of tea. She shook her head, watching as Mary Jane wrapped a handful of cookies in a napkin.

She climbed the stairs, thinking of Uncle Ben. Just the day before, at this very hour, he was going up and down the same steps, waving to her from the porch. Just hours ago, he was looking at the carpet, maybe wondering if they should do something about the worn patch on the edge of the steps.

Peter's door was closed. She would just go in there and wait for him—he's probably not far behind. Maybe he caught the next bus.

She opened the door slowly...and there he was. Lying on his bed, hands linked behind his head and staring at the ceiling.

"Peter!"

He jumped. "Mary Jane!"

"What are you doing here?"

"This is my room."

Now he sat up fully. His eyes were red, but other than that he looked normal.

There's absolutely no way he could have made it back here before me! Spider-Man was going in the other direction!

So there was only one logical explanation: Peter was NOT Spider-Man. For some reason that knowledge disappointed her, but just for a moment. There were far more important things to think about.

"Peter." She sat next to him and put the bundle of cookies on his knee. "Here. Eat something."

He gave her a weak smile. "That's a switch. You telling me to eat."

"I know. But look—they have those little pink layer cookies you used to love so much."

He shook his head. "Nah. I'm fine." But his face was anything but fine.

She slipped her arm around him, surprised by the solid feel of his muscles. He slowly put his arm around her waist. Wordlessly, they sat for a few minutes.

He turned his head towards her, resting against the crook of her neck. "It's my fault."

"No it's not. How could it be your fault?"

"The other night, after the wrestling match, I saw this guy. I could have stopped him. I knew he was a petty criminal, he had some lady's purse in his hand and he was running. But I did nothing. I could have tripped him, called 911, anything. But I didn't. I was pissed at the world and turned the other way."

"Peter, the police say it was a random crime. I'm sure it wasn't the same guy."

He shook his head. "How do I know that? And even if it wasn't, what's to stop that guy from going out and hurting someone else? Someone else's mother, or father, or...uncle? I'll tell you what *could* have stopped him. Me."

"Oh, Peter." Mary Jane felt a deep sadness. "You can't undo what's already happened. Trust me, I know all about it. When my dad..." her voice caught, and she felt Peter's arm tighten around her middle. "When my dad left my mom and me, I thought it was my fault. I really did."

"That's crazy, MJ. You were like, eight years old."

"I was a very mature 9, thank you," she smiled a little. "But when you're a kid, you don't know that. All you know is one day your dad's there, the next night, he's not. I've spent I don't know how many nights wondering what I might have done to drive him away. Still do, sometimes." She picked at a threadbare patch on his comforter.

"The point is, I get it now. He's not coming back. Ever. And I'll never really know if it was my fault or not. All I can do is not let it mess me up too much, right?" As she spoke, she looked up, straight at Peter, desperate for him to understand.

He stared back at her. Then nodded. "Right."

"Don't be so hard on yourself, Peter. I know you. You'll do the right thing next time," she said. There was no doubt in her mind this was true.

"With great power comes great responsibility," he said softly.

"Who said that?"

"My dad. It's something Uncle Ben told me."

Mary Jane repeated it to herself, thinking about her run-in with Harry, how she had led him on to get what she wanted. It had never occurred to her that it would get her into such trouble. Or that anyone, least of all Harry, would get hurt in the process.

Suddenly Peter reached out and hugged her, hugged her close. "Thank you."

"For what?" She rubbed his back, and he took a deep breath.

"Just...thanks."

Then he frowned, and peered at her. "Mary Jane, your tongue is orange. Have you been drinking OZ?"

"No. Just orange soda." Then she shrugged. "Nevermind. It's a long story. But I think we should go downstairs now. Your Aunt May needs you."

He closed his eyes, as if willing the strength to do what she said. Then he opened them, and looked directly at Mary Jane. "You're right. Okay." He stood up, then reached out his hand and pulled her to her feet. "Do I look okay? I mean, do I look as if I've been crying or anything?"

"You look great, Peter. Really." And she meant it.

"Okay." He walked to the door and turned to her. "How about a little sweet and sour liver soufflé?"

"I think I'll pass."

Together they faced the crowd below.

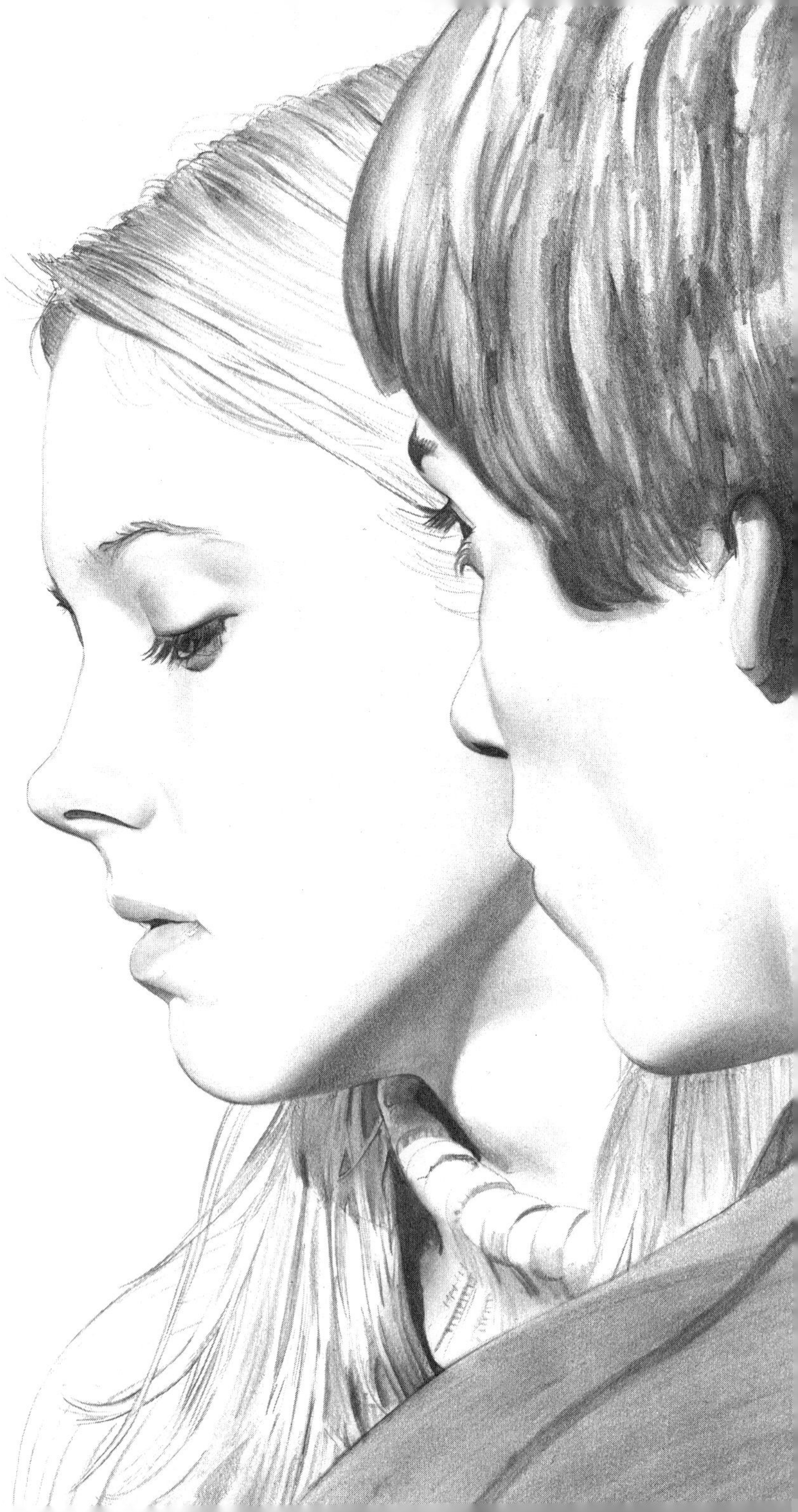

# chapter 9

For the first time in weeks, maybe months, Mary Jane was home for dinner. She could have stayed at the Parkers'. But she had a strange urge to go home, to see her mother.

Maybe it was just being at a house in mourning. Or being with a family, a real family. It occurred to her, as she watched Peter help Aunt May, and Aunt May's expression as she looked at Peter, that a family wasn't about numbers. Or genders. Just because a father, or father-figure, was gone did not make them any less of a family. They were diminished, perhaps. But they were still a family.

That was her problem. Ever since her father left, Mary Jane had felt as if she lived with fragments—bits and pieces of what had been, remainders of what will never again be. Yet that distinction had been mostly in her mind, not in reality.

Aunt May said something that evening. "Life is about change, Mary Jane. Some of it good, some of it bad." She had continued that both she and Ben knew they were old, and that one of them was bound to go first. While she wasn't prepared for what had happened—how could anyone be?—she was secure that he had loved her and Peter. That could never be taken away.

Maybe her own father had loved her, in his own way. Maybe he still loved her, even if he no longer felt he could live with them.

As Aunt May said, life is about change.

Her mother was in the kitchen when she came home. "Hi, Mom." Something smelled delicious. And since the TV was off, she knew Mike was not there.

"Mary Jane!" Her mom was wearing an apron. "How is Peter doing, and his aunt?"

"They're still in shock, I think. But they are strong. It will be difficult, but they'll be okay."

"I'll make them some brownies or something."

"They'd appreciate that."

Her mother started back to the kitchen, then she paused. "Don't you have cheerleading practice?"

She braced herself. "No. I quit."

"Oh. Well, that's your decision."

"But I didn't tell you yesterday—I got a full scholarship to the Manhattan School of Ballet."

"You did? Oh, honey, I'm so happy for you!"

And she seemed genuinely happy, not her usual fake happy.

"Do you think Granny pulled some strings, or even paid for the lessons?"

Madeline Watson shook her head. "No, I don't think so. She was delighted to have you take ballet when you were little, but believe me, the last thing she wants is to see her only granddaughter go into show business!"

Mary Jane laughed. "Ballet as show business? I've never thought of it as that."

"Trust me on this, she has. The only good thing about us moving to Queens was that there was less chance of you becoming too involved with dance. She told me that. It was the bright spot in her life, and almost made up for having a Skye Bleu salesgal for an ex-daughter-in-law."

"I'm not that good anyway," she went into the kitchen and lifted the lid of a pan. "Wow, that looks great!"

"I was hoping to tempt you. Those are Swedish meatballs. You used to love them as a kid." Then she stepped closer and pushed the hair out of her daughter's eyes. "And you are good, Mary Jane. Better than good. I don't think I've ever seen a dancer like you at such a young age. And I've seen them all, Gelsey Kirkland and Leslie Browne. Hundreds of dancers that come and go, usually go with one twist of an ankle. Even Margot Fonteyn. But you've always had something else. Something special."

"Really? Mom, you never said anything like that before."

Madeline shrugged and stirred the meatballs. "Honey, I was afraid."

"Afraid of what?"

"That you'd get hurt. That the life of a dancer would be too hard on you. That if you did something like cheerleading, you'd have a chance to land a better husband. Not some guy in pink tights."

Mary Jane smiled. "I love ballet, but I don't know if I'd want to make it my life, even if I was good enough. And believe me, this cheerleading squad isn't likely to win any beauty contests."

"I'm just happy for you. You deserve all the good things that come your way."

They hadn't spoken like this for so long, maybe never. It was a risk, but it was one she had to take. "Mom, you deserve good things, too. You really do."

"Thank you, dear." The curtain was about to close again. Mary Jane could feel it.

"This is none of my business, I know that. But...I mean, you deserve better than Mike."

There. She said it.

Her mother checked the flame on the stove and stirred the pot. "I know I do," she said off-handedly.

"I'm serious." Maybe she shouldn't press, but she had to. She'd never forgive herself if she let the opportunity slip away. "Mom, he's a real creep."

"I know, dear."

"I don't think you do. Not really." Should she

mention they way he looks at her, at Mary Jane? Or how he tried to grab her?

"Give me some credit, dear. I've dumped his sorry rear-end."

Did her mother just say that? "You what?"

"He's a loser. Do you want salad with dinner?"

Mary Jane blinked. "Yeah, sure. Mom, when did this happen?"

"Yesterday. And I feel as if I've lost a hundred and eighty pounds of flabby beer gut. Italian or Russian?"

"Italian or Russian?"

"Dressing for the salad."

"Italian. Yeah, Italian would be good. When did you decide this?"

"Oh, Mary Jane," she sighed and put down the wooden spoon. "I don't know. All my life I thought a woman needs a man. Not only for financial security, but to form her identity. To show the world who she is, and where her rightful place is in that world. But even when I was with your father, nothing was secure. We moved out here, and suddenly I was making the money. I was the head of the household. And I realized that Mike was just an old habit, an old bad habit, like smoking. He was making my life—our life—worse, not better. I'd rather feel healthy without a man than sick with one. And Mary Jane, as you said often, Mike was one sick puppy."

Mary Jane blinked in astonishment. "Are you okay? I mean, can I do anything?"

"Yes, hon. Could you slice the cucumbers for the salad?"

Then her mother reached out and touched her shoulder. "We'll be fine, Mary Jane. Really we will."

"I know," she whispered.

* * *

After dinner Mary Jane examined the papers from Harry's house.

It was all there, in a classified memo! OZ was, indeed, a highly addictive performance enhancer whose key ingredient possessed a lactic-acid inhibitor and a chemical additive that worked not unlike anabolic steroids. One test subject, some guy in Germany, according to a memo, had actually gone bonkers after overdosing on the stuff and killed everyone in the lab. Another assistant, a woman, ended up setting herself on fire in a playground.

Why was Norman Osborn doing this?

A few scraps of paper made that answer clear. The money. OZ was incredibly inexpensive to make. And once people were hooked on the stuff, they'd do anything to get more. He could put it on the market, make a quick killing, then withdraw it, claiming he had no idea it was harmful.

Norman Osborn was willing to destroy countless lives—including that of his own son—for a fat bank account.

"Sick," she muttered to herself.

Then an idea came to her. About the school project they were working on. And even though it had been a long day, she ran to the phone and called Peter.

* * *

Miss Ingram was shocked that Peter Parker and Mary Jane Watson were the first team to complete the science project.

"Peter, you do realize you could have had an extension," she said gently.

Their final project, a detailed analysis of the biodegradable dishwashing detergent Aunt May favored, earned Mary Jane and Peter a B+.

But the science projects were quickly forgotten once the city's major newspaper, the *Daily Bugle*, broke the biggest scandal of the year: Osborn Industries' Founder Norman Osborn Accused of Endangering Local Youths: Illegal Use of Controlled Substances in OZ Sports Drink Suspected.

The news article, already being hailed as Pulitzer Prize material for its investigative journalism, cited as its key piece of evidence a classified memo that circulated only within senior-level management at Osborn Industries. It came from an anonymous source.

* * *

By late afternoon, policemen and biochemists were swarming Midtown High, collecting samples of OZ and interviewing students and teachers. Camera crews arrived. Mary Jane saw Miss Downey burst into tears while being quizzed by a detective.

Mary Jane and Peter watched with fascination.

"Wow. We did this, MJ. We caused all this."

"I know," she said in wonderment. "You do think we did the right thing, don't you?"

"We did what we had to do."

"I just feel bad for Harry."

"Yeah, me too. But what else could we have done?" The question hung in the air between them, and neither had an answer.

*   *   *

After school, Mary Jane caught up with Peter. Something had been on her mind all day, and despite the incredible events of the past few days, this made her more nervous than anything else. "Um, Peter?"

"Yeah?"

"Tomorrow night...I was wondering..." Her mouth was suddenly dry. "Would you like to go to the movies or something?"

He stumbled over his own feet. "Excuse me?"

"I said, would you like to go to the movies?" Her face flushed.

"With you?"

"No, with Flash Thompson. Of course with me." She held her breath.

"Well, it's Uncle Ben's funeral tomorrow."

Mary Jane felt incredibly stupid. "I'm sorry. Of course you won't be in any kind of mood for a movie."

"It's in the morning. But later should be all right. The last thing I want to do is sit at home and feel sorry for myself. Besides..."

"Besides what?"

"Aunt May says she won't let me in the house until after ten. She's booting me, her way of trying to help me, I guess. So I have nowhere else to go."

"Great," she sighed, relieved. She'd never asked a guy out before. Then she remembered something. "I have my first ballet class in Manhattan tomorrow afternoon."

"That's right—I forgot all about that! Are you psyched?"

"Yes. I mean, I'm incredibly psyched. But the class doesn't end until eight or so. Would that be too late?"

"Perfect. Two hour movie, and I can get in the front door if it's after ten."

A date. A date with Peter?

Perfect.

* * *

The news stunned the nation, not just New York. The massive plot. The kids at a major metropolitan high school used as guinea pigs. Norman Osborn being led away in handcuffs.

"My God," Mary Jane watched the news. Footage of Coach Renny ringing his hands. Scenes of kids with bright blue tongues. And for a quick second, Mary Jane saw herself and Peter hanging in the background of one of the camera pans.

The phone rang, and it was Peter. "Are you watching this?"

"I can't believe this. It can't be happening."

"I know, I'm going over to Harry's. I feel so terrible for him. Do you want me to pick you up?"

"Not now. I just can't see him right now." She didn't want to explain any more, and he didn't ask. "Maybe he just needs you. I mean, you're his closest friend. Probably his only friend now."

And when they hung up, she realized that now there was no reason to worry about OZ anymore. It was all gone, as was Harry's father, probably for life.

As was Harry's own life as he knew it. Poor guy. Soon he, too, would have to adjust to an entirely different world. She tried to think about Norman Osborn and his careless disregard for life—for Peter's life, even for that of his own son. She reminded herself that Norman Osborn was the wrong-doer, and that she and Peter had simply caught him in the act.

Then why did she feel so lousy?

Aunt May had said it best, life is about change. Some of it good, some of it bad.

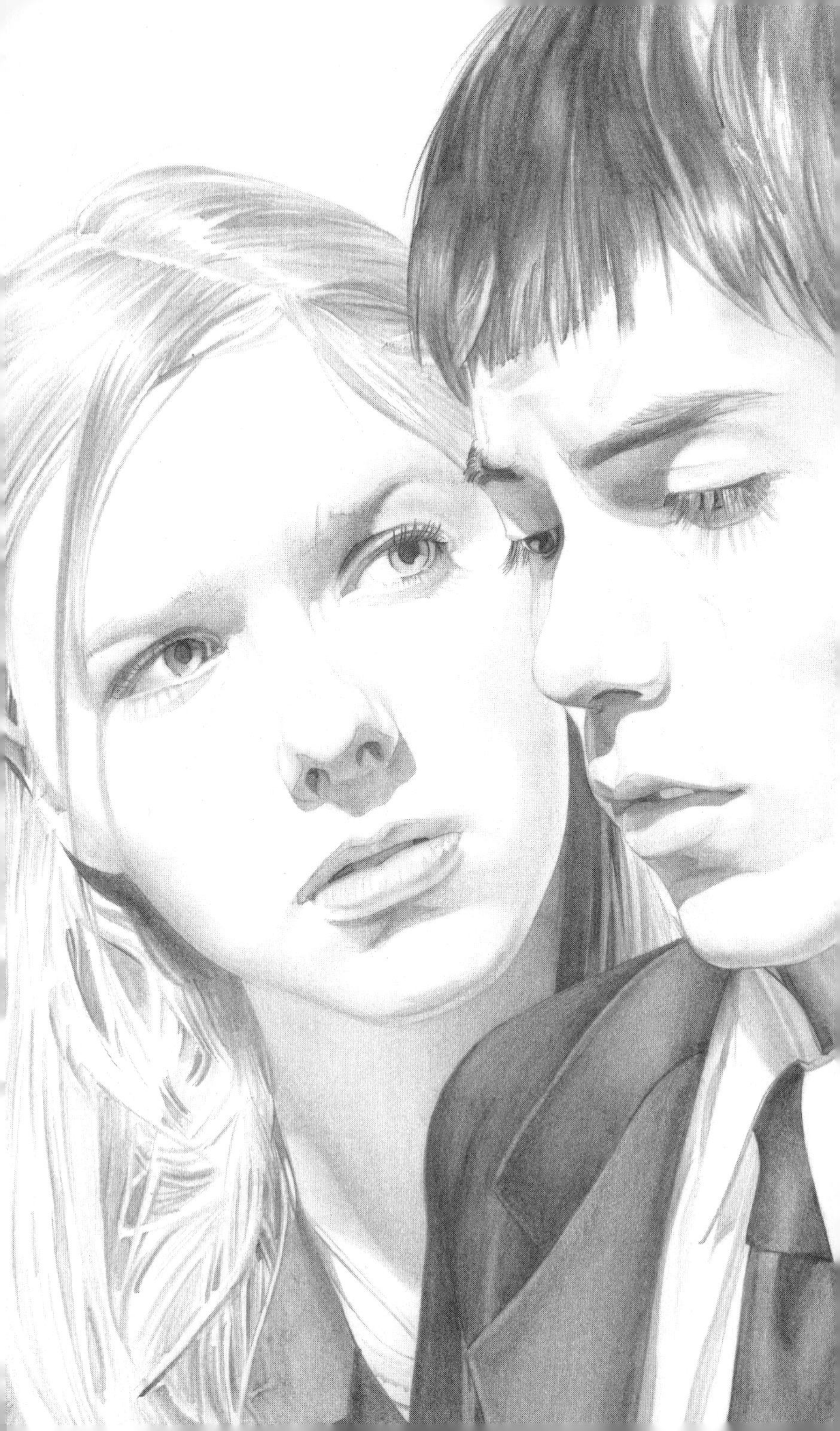

# chapter 10

Ben Parker's funeral was held on an incongruously sunny Saturday, the kind of day that usually calls for picnics and long bicycle rides and walks in the park. Instead there were clusters of black-clad mourners with perplexed expressions on their faces, still confused about how something so violent and final could happen to a man so gentle and giving.

Harry Osborn did not attend the funeral. He had his own sorrow to address, his own shame and confusion. Despite the weekend, many of the kids from school were there, along with their teachers. Although few of them actually knew Ben Parker, dozens turned out to join in a sense of community mourning.

Peter and Aunt May sat on folded chairs at the cemetery, watching with hollow eyes as the minister tossed a clump of dirt on the polished oak casket. A bright green artificial grass tarp surrounded the coffin and the freshly dug grave. Just beyond the site was a yellow plow manned by a solitary worker in a tee-shirt. Mary Jane watched the man as he waited with some impatience for the service to end, for the people to leave so he could finish his job and push Uncle Ben into the ground.

Peter stared straight ahead, his shoulders squared, wearing one of Uncle Ben's old suit jackets. Aunt May held a lace handkerchief to her face, dabbing at tears that had rolled over her cheek with deliberation, as if she could dab away the pain. Sometimes she would look over at Peter, who would break his straight-ahead stare long enough to pat her hand and smile weakly.

At last the service was over.

"Are you going back to the Parkers'?" Wendy asked.

Mary Jane shook her head. "No. I have ballet class."

"You're kidding? I mean, you've known Peter for like a million years. I'm not saying this just because I feel incredibly awkward eating chicken salad at some dead guy's house without you, but don't you think you should come? Out of respect for his uncle and all that."

Mary Jane watched Peter stand slowly, guiding Aunt May to her feet before shaking hands with the minister.

"Um, yeah. I thought I should go, but Peter insisted I go to ballet. He said it would look bad at the school if I miss the first day. And we're catching a movie later tonight anyway."

Wendy's eyes widened. "A movie? As in a date?"

"Not really," she shrugged. "We're just getting together."

"I see." For the first time that day Wendy grinned. "Just getting together in a dark theater. On a Saturday night. Date night."

"Well, I don't think it's..." Then Mary Jane paused. "You know what, Wendy? I don't really know what the heck is going on. I mean, is it a date? Two old friends and science project partners catching a flick? Or is it something else? I don't know. But it sure felt like a date when I asked him."

"*You* asked him out? Damn, girl..." Wendy's eyes widened with respect.

Just then Peter looked over at the two girls, and then at Mary Jane. A flash of understanding lit his face, and she knew—she just knew—he understood that Wendy was once again her friend and confidant. He winked at her, a gesture so swift she almost missed it. He turned away when a woman in an oversized black hat pressed something into his hand.

"I think I know exactly what the heck is going on." Wendy glanced around at the people leaving in clusters. "Oh, MJ, there's Meg and Belinda. Mind if I head on out with them? I mean, if you're going to ballet and all."

"Nah, go ahead. And enjoy the chicken salad."

"Sure. I'll save you some. Call me later, okay? When you get back from the movies. If you're alone, that is. Catch my drift?"

"Subtle as a train wreck, Wendy. Yeah. I'll call."

Wendy ran off to catch up with the other girls. A chilly breeze swept across the sloping lawn, and Mary Jane crossed her arms against the coldness.

With one final glance at Uncle Ben's casket, at Peter surrounded by a crowd of well-wishers, Mary Jane left the cemetery.

* * *

The Manhattan School of Ballet was a different universe.

It wasn't simply one of the best dance schools in the country. There were fine dance schools all over the place, from Mikeas to Idaho. But the Manhattan School of Ballet was a large complex of studios that churned out some of the most magnificent dancers in the world. To even take a class there indicated a level of expertise that was far beyond your run-of-the-mill schools.

This was no Ruby's House-O-Dance.

Mary Jane scurried into the high-ceilinged studio on the fifth floor. A stunning view of Lincoln Center was offset by walls of mirrors.

It had grown since she had been a student there. There were more studios, a new wing with an incredible sound system in the ceiling.

It smelled of dance, of backstage. There was a bustle, a hurry and excitement there. The other dancers, pale and serious, tied the ribbons on their worn pink satin toe shoes as they chatted or stretched or checked their turn-outs in the mirror.

The large double door opened, and in strode Yuri Ivanovich. Mary Jane's jaw dropped.

Yuri Inanovich! Generally considered to be the finest dancer on the planet! His defection from the former Soviet Union had nearly caused a war! She had heard he was teaching now, but never in a million years had she expected him to be teaching her class.

"Okay, kids," he clapped his hands, and everyone scurried to the barre. The piano player struck a single cord.

Wasn't he one of the piano players with the Philharmonic? She had seen him in a free concert in Central Park a few years ago.

Then class began.

Her initial terror at not being able to keep up vanished. She glanced at the mirror, at the row of dancers performing the same exercises at the same time, and she was one of them. She fit in.

Yuri Ivanovich strolled down the barre, adjusting an elbow here, clicking about an uneven shoulder there. She heard the tone of his familiar voice. How many times had she seen him in movies, or interviewed on TV?

He was scolding a student now, really chewing her out. The girl tried to keep going, tried to do as he instructed even as she battled tears.

"Turn-out!" He clapped his hands. "That is no turn-out!"

From a distance Mary Jane could see the girl struggle for control, attempting to do exactly as told and remain unruffled. But she couldn't.

"You are no dancer," he said harshly. "You should know that now."

The room was suddenly still.

The music began again. Mary Jane shook off the image of the girl down the barre. And within an instant she was lost in the moment, the blessed music mingling with the ballet. Her eyes followed her fingertips as she opened to second, feeling like a blossoming flower. Floating on air, as if on a cloud, she felt as if the music was deep in her bones. She felt as if she was the music, dance.

"Very nice," Yuri Ivanovich said to her before moving on.

Very nice! Yuri Ivanovich said her movements were very nice!

Mary Jane let out the breath she was barely aware she'd been holding.

At last she was home.

* * *

"Excuse me," she asked the woman at the desk after class.

The woman in the cat's-eye glasses looked up from her computer. "Yes?"

"Excuse me, but I'm a new student."

"Is there a problem?"

"No, no problem. I mean, it's great. It's wonderful!

But I'm here on some sort of scholarship. Is there any way to find out why?"

The woman seemed surprised. "Did a scout come to any of your previous dance classes?"

Mary Jane shook her head. "No. That's why I'm confused. I just received a letter offering a full scholarship."

"That's most unusual." The woman clicked a few keys. "Name?"

"Watson, Mary Jane."

She clicked, typing quickly, her eyes focused on the screen.

"Here you are. Hm. Interesting."

"What is it?"

"You used to be a student here, right?"

"Yes. Years ago when I was a little kid."

"Well, there's not much information listed. Just that a benefactor who wishes to remain anonymous has paid for a full year of unlimited lessons."

"So is this a scholarship?"

"Sort of, but not really. Let's just put it this way: whoever did this has tremendous faith in your abilities."

"Could it be my grandmother?"

The woman shook her head. "I doubt it. Grandmothers usually want to take all the credit they can. Trust me."

"Is there any way for me to find out who this mysterious person is?"

"Nope. They even paid in cash."

"Cash?"

"Cash. Something new and different these days."

"Okay. Thank you."

She was about to leave when she saw the girl who had been yelled at in class, hunched over in a chair. She hadn't bothered to take off her leotard. Her hair was still pulled back into a painful bun, a lank ribbon dangling on one side.

Mary Jane hesitated for just an instant. Then she stepped over. "Hey, are you all right?"

The girl sniffed and looked up. "No. I'm not. I should just give it up and...Mary Jane Watson?"

"Yeah!"

"It's me, Amanda Peterson!"

"Oh my God, Amanda! How are you?"

"Terrible. But that's just because I suck at ballet. I can't believe it's you! I saw you and Pukey Parker all over CNN this afternoon!"

"Are you still at Bradford?"

"Yeah. As if my parents would let me go anyplace else. I hate it. I really do. Jeez, Mary Jane, I can't believe it's you!"

She shrugged, not quite sure how to take Amanda's reaction.

"I also can't believe Yuri complimented you. Do you know how I'd kill for just one measly 'Very nice?' I believe I'd kill for less than that. A lot less. Where have you been taking? I mean, you're so good!"

Is she kidding? Is she setting me up for one of her

nasty tricks, just for old time's sake?

"I've been studying at Ruby's House-O-Dance. Queens Boulevard."

"Oh. Well, they must be fantastic. Hey, maybe we can have dinner after class next time?"

Mary Jane tried to see if she was joking. But this Amanda seemed so different from the Queen Bee of elementary school days. Now she seemed vulnerable. Almost fragile. Dark circles under her damp eyes. Her complexion was sallow.

"Sure, dinner would be great," she said uncertainly.

"Listen, Mary Jane, it is really wonderful to see you. I mean, well..." She leaned over and hugged her. "It's just wonderful to see you."

Slightly dazed, Mary Jane nodded and stumbled over to the subway. The moment she got home she called Peter. He picked up on the first ring.

"You'll never guess who's in my ballet class! Amanda Peterson!"

"You're kidding!" He sounded out of breath. "Listen. They caught him."

She knew at once who he was talking about. The guy who killed Uncle Ben. "How? I mean..."

"It's a long story. Hey, is it too late to get together?"

"Tonight?"

"Yeah, tonight."

She thought for a moment. "I don't know. It took longer than I thought to get home tonight. It's too late for a movie. Are you hungry? Why don't you come over and I'll make us something to eat."

He paused. "You know, that sounds great. I really feel like I've got to get out of here. Sure it's okay with your mom?"

"I'm sure. Just come over as soon as possible."

"Yeah, I will. And MJ?"

"Yes?"

"Thanks."

Mary Jane turned to find her mother standing in the hallway, tying her bathrobe. "How was ballet?"

"Oh, Mom. It was wonderful. I'll tell you more about it later on. Is it okay if Peter comes over?"

"Um, well, it's a little late. But I guess it's fine. Are you hungry?"

"Yup. I'm starving. I'll make something for me and Peter." Mary Jane stepped into the kitchen and began opening the cupboards.

Her mother followed, then smiled. "It's so good to have you back, hon."

"I was only at dance class."

"That's not what I meant. Good night, Mary Jane. And say hello to Peter for me."

By the time she turned around, her mother already gone.

And then she saw exactly the can she was looking for. With only a vague idea of what she was doing, she began to prepare dinner.

Peter knocked softly on the door, not wanting to wake up the other neighbors.

"Hey," she said as she let him in.

"Hey. Um, the deli was closed."

Mary Jane looked at him. "I am very sorry to hear that," she said uncertainly.

"No, what I mean is I wanted to get you some flowers. You know how they sell flowers on the side, next to the fruit stand?"

"Oh, sure. You don't have to bring me flowers. But thank you for the thought."

He shrugged and took off his jacket. "I brought some other stuff," he handed her a shopping bag.

"Peter, you shouldn't have..." Then she saw that on top was her red and blue tights and leotard.

"Yeah. Um, you left those over a long time ago. Kept on forgetting to give them back to you."

She held them up, and they were hopelessly stretched out of shape. "Who wore these, King Kong?"

"No, I guess Aunt May washed them. Maybe she shouldn't have used hot water."

"It was nice of her to wash them," she placed them on a chair. "What else is in here?"

"Some potato chips and pretzels. And that's chicken salad in the plastic container. We had a lot left over."

"Oh, great." She put the food on the counter.

"Peter, how was it?"

"Pretty weird. Father Perkins got ripped on apple brandy. I found someone's teeth in a glass of celery tonic."

"I mean, how are you?"

"Fine, I guess." He looked down. "I don't know. Glad they caught the guy. Glad the day is over. I don't know how I feel anymore."

Without thinking she stepped toward him and took his hand. It was surprisingly large, his hand, and warm. Slowly he raised his head.

A riot of emotions coursed through her at that moment. Empathy. Friendship. A deep sense of belonging. A sense of wishing to share everything with the person right next to her. And there was something else, something new and confusing and wonderful.

Passion?

"Mary Jane." His breath ruffled her hair.

She swallowed. "Peter."

Languidly he leaned to her, and pressed his lips to hers.

She slipped a hand up his arm, and then on the back of his neck. And the kiss deepened, sweet and inevitable as a sigh.

Then he pulled back, his face widening into a grin. "Something smells good."

Returning the smile, she stroked the collar of his shirt. "It's tuna casserole. The only thing missing was the potato chips for the top. And you brought them."

"Yeah, well. There are a few mashed cheese doodles mixed in."

"Nice touch."

"Yeah, sure is."

Again they kissed, less tentatively this time. Both still very aware this was new and a little frightening. After this, their friendship would never be the same.

"I'll bet this will be the best casserole I've ever had," he whispered.

"I hope so."

It was.

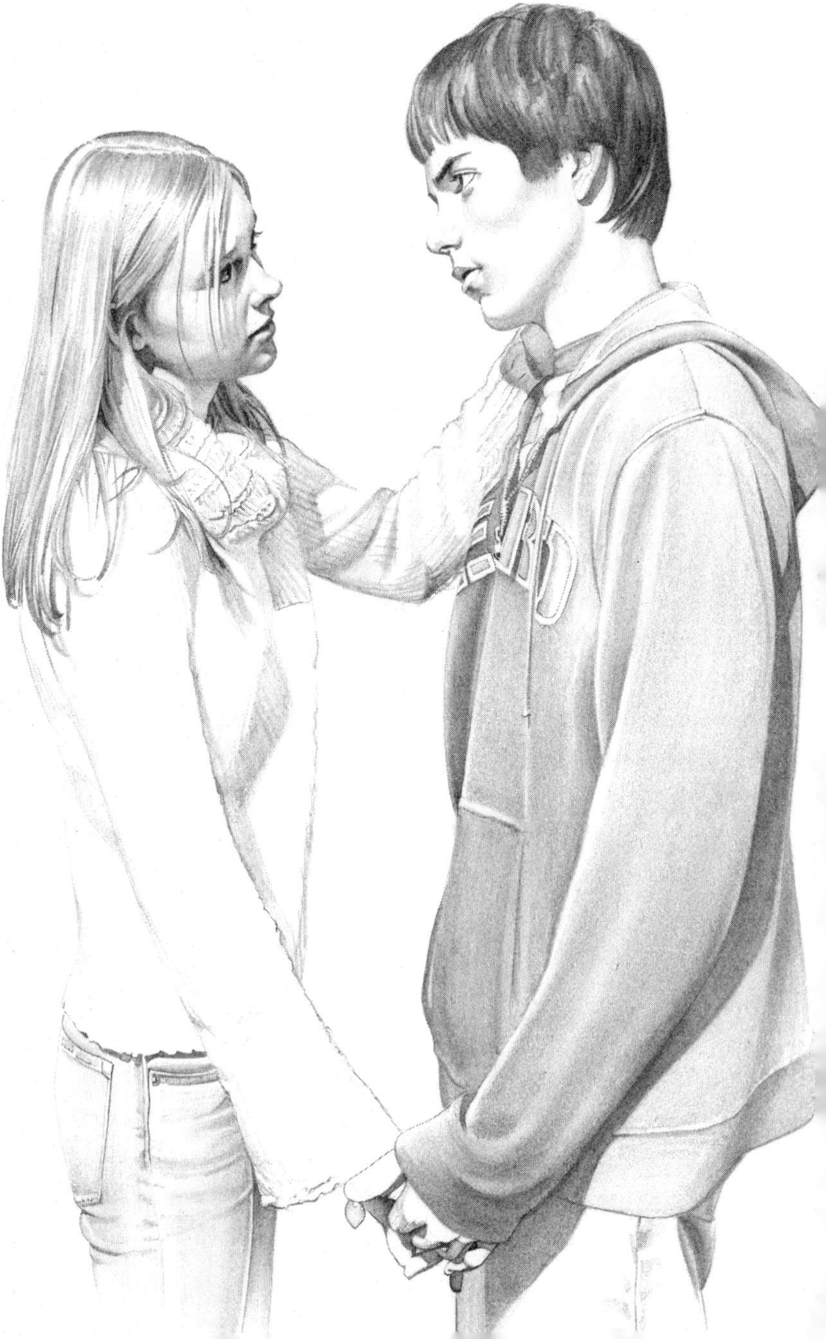